TRUST AND FOLLOW JESUS

CONVERSATIONS
TO FUEL DISCIPLESHIP

BOBBY HARRINGTON
WITH CARL AND ALICIA WILLIAMSON

To Cindy—
My beautiful wife, inside and out.
The first draft of this book was written in your honor,
so many years ago.
Now it is formally dedicated to you
as we celebrate forty years of marriage this year.
Thank you for the great privilege you have bestowed on me
by being my wife, friend, lover, fellow sufferer,
chief advocate, and co-minister in the gospel.

RENEW

RENEWING THE TEACHINGS OF JESUS
TO FUEL DISCIPLE MAKING

RENEW.ORG

CONTENTS

PREFACE..................................9

INTRODUCTION AND HOW TO USE THIS MANUAL.....................11

CHAPTER 1: God...............17

CHAPTER 2: Jesus in History.....................31

CHAPTER 3: Scripture..................37

CHAPTER 4: God Is Holy.....................45

CHAPTER 5: God Is Love.....................53

CHAPTER 6: Lord and King.....................63

CHAPTER 7: Commitment.....................71

CHAPTER 8: Discipleship...................79

APPENDIX I: Transformation Group Resources.....................87

APPENDIX II: Three Classic Arguments for God's Existence.....................95

ENDNOTES...................101

ABOUT THE AUTHORS...................105

The material that you will find in this book is designed to introduce newcomers to the core teachings of the faith and provide meaningful conversation for mature disciples. It is intended to teach a gospel message that is so compelling (and biblical) that it leads to discipleship. We believe the gospel we preach and the Jesus we present determines the kind of disciple a person becomes.

Thus, the goal of this material is to establish authentic disciples whose minds are informed, hearts are enflamed, and hands are activated by the gospel of Jesus Christ. It is for you to process in a smaller, relational setting.

There are three keys to remember as you embark on a plan to go over this material with others:

1. **Life on Life.** We cannot state strongly enough that the goal is to cover this material in a life-on-life context, as opposed to solely an educational one. The format is designed for open, honest sharing together. Please set the example each time for others by sharing your personal reflections. Invite one another into your lives outside the group. Pray for each other, text each other, and talk often. We want to follow and be like Jesus, who invited those he was discipling into a relationship with him that encompassed all of life.

2. **Meet weekly; keep it small and gender-based.** We recommend that you meet weekly in a relational place, such as a coffee shop or in a home. Ideally, you will start with two to four other people of the same gender in your meeting. As you will see in the introductory chapter (and Appendix I), each of the groups will start—after forming a covenant—with each person's spiritual biography. This path of first getting to know each other will help you start with a strong relational tone. Once you finish the spiritual autobiographies, work through each chapter of this book and keep the number of meetings on this material to eight, which is vitally important in church contexts where people will be reviewing this material annually.

3. **Review the questions and read the chapter before each meeting.** The format of the study is for people to read the material before the meetings so that you can discuss your answers to the questions. If you do not read the material before you meet, plan on at least an hour and a half for your meeting time.

Need more in-depth background? The leader's guide for this book, which gives background material that answers questions about each chapter, is available on Amazon.com—see Bobby Harrington, *Trust and Follow Jesus: The Leader's Guide.*

I hope and pray that this book will help you to trust and follow Jesus and help others join you in that grand quest.

—Bobby Harrington with Carl and Alicia Williamson

INTRODUCTION AND HOW TO USE THIS MANUAL

This book is meant to help people be disciples of Jesus and make other disciples of Jesus.

Any manual designed to help us model Jesus-style disciple making should begin with Jesus. He tells his disciples not to be anxious about life, for the Father already knows our needs. For this reason, disciples of Jesus are able to focus on seeking "first the kingdom of God and his righteousness" (Matthew 6:33, ESV). Again, the goal of this material is to establish authentic disciples whose minds are informed, whose hearts are enflamed, and whose hands are activated by the gospel of Jesus Christ.

Jesus names God's plan for the world by interpreting the Law of Moses, the Prophets, and Psalms:

> Then he opened their minds to understand the Scriptures, and said to them, "Thus it is written, that the Christ should suffer and on the third day rise from the dead, and that repentance for the forgiveness of sins should be proclaimed in his name to all nations, beginning from Jerusalem. You are witnesses of these things. And behold, I am sending the promise [the Holy Spirit] of my Father upon you. But stay in the city until you are clothed with power [the Holy Spirit] from on high." (Luke 24:45–49, ESV)

The historic Park Street Church in downtown Boston was established in 1809 with a 217-foot steeple that stands as a reminder that the church points the way to God. The building contains large windows that illustrate the contrast between life and death.[1] Likewise, God utilizes the church (the people of God, not the building) to point to him through Jesus Christ in the power of the Holy Spirit. We stand as witnesses of those who have gone from death to life. We have risen from the dead and now proclaim repentance for the forgiveness of sins to all nations.

Following the pattern of the day of Pentecost in Acts 2, it would take approximately 7,209 years to reach all nations, assuming a population of 7.9 billion people and a conversion of 3,000 lost souls being baptized into the name of Jesus *every day*. Nevertheless, relational disciple making groups of four people would reach the entire world in thirty-one years if they multiplied to form two groups of four after one year, and if each of those groups continuously multiplied.

- Year 0: 1 person invites 3 people to join together in relational and intentional disciple making (4 people total)
- Year 1: 2 groups of 4 people (8 people total)
- Year 2: 4 groups of 4 people (16 people total)
- Year 3: 8 groups of 4 people (32 people total)
- Year 4: 16 groups of 4 people (64 people total)
- Year 5: 32 groups of 4 people (128 people total)
- Year 10: 1,024 groups of 4 people (4,096 people total)
- Year 20: 1,048,576 groups of 4 people (4,194,304 people total)
- Year 30: 1,073,741,824 groups of 4 people (4,294,967,296 people total)
- Year 31: 2,147,483,648 groups of 4 people (8,589,934,592 people total)

The reality of God's kingdom is that he calls *every disciple of Jesus* to invite people into a relational—yet counter-cultural—mindset based on the truth of Jesus; the divine inspiration and authority of the Bible; the holiness and love of God; the importance of repentance, confession, and baptism in conversion; the call to a faithful life; and discipleship in the local church.

This workbook is designed to train and multiply disciple makers. The Bible is our curriculum for learning to live and love like Jesus. We want people to become disciples or to grow stronger as disciples with rock-solid convictions. We believe that fear and uncertainty has prevented many followers of Jesus from being fruitful in making and maturing disciples. For this reason, this manual provides clear instructions on how to train disciples in the values and rhythms of Jesus-style disciple making, and it provides a starting place for walking through the gospel of Jesus Christ. In each chapter, we will look at what God desires everyday disciples to learn and re-learn so that we can truly trust and follow Jesus today in joyful submission.

> THIS WORKBOOK IS DESIGNED TO TRAIN AND MULTIPLY DISCIPLE MAKERS.

This manual is designed to be utilized by followers of Jesus who desire to multiply disciples and disciple makers. Jesus-style disciple making is the best method to replicate. Therefore, we have sought to identify three strategic values and four rhythms of Jesus. This model should neither replace nor stand in the way of the work of the Holy Spirit in making disciples who make disciples. Instead, the disciple making model outlined below is a type of scaffolding to encourage faithful followers of Jesus to mature as disciple makers.

Have you ever read Matthew, Mark, Luke, and John with this question in mind: *How did Jesus make disciples who make disciples?*[2] What did he do in his everyday relationships with the twelve men he invited along in his ministry? He worked with three key values and modeled four recurring, relational rhythms (both Kingdom Teachings and Kingdom Doings) in his disciple-making efforts. We see the church, as early as Acts 2:42–47, imitating Jesus in these values and rhythms, and we also should imitate him in our groups today.

HOW DID JESUS MAKE DISCIPLES WHO MAKE DISCIPLES?

Three Strategic Values

1. **Prayer and Fasting**: Jesus was moved by the power of the Holy Spirit and grounded in fasting and prayer with his heavenly Father (Matthew 4:1–11; See also Acts 2:42, 47).

   Fast and pray for your group and with your group—as if for your own children!

2. **Inviting Along**: Jesus actively loved people, and he invited along those who welcomed him into their lives to love God and others with him (Matthew 4:19; See also Acts 2:42, 44, 46).

   Disciple making involves a specific invitation to do life together. Relationships, Relationships, Relationships.

3. **Multiplication**: Jesus matured his disciples while instilling multiplication as an integral part of their disciple making DNA (Matthew 4:19; See also Acts 2:47).

   From the beginning, multiplication is an expectation. We believe the most effective way to multiply is by having groups of four and continuously multiplying by a factor of two.

Four Disciple Making Rhythms

In order to model our disciple making in a way that seeks first God's kingdom and righteousness, we not only want to value the things that Jesus values, but we also model our rhythms after his.

WE WANT TO BECOME PEOPLE WHO ARE INTENTIONALLY TRAINING DISCIPLE MAKERS.

Disciple making takes intentionality and relationship. We want to become people who are intentionally training disciple makers, and that requires growing in our knowledge of God *and* living out his teachings in the world. That is why these four rhythms fall under two categories: "Kingdom Teachings" (see Matthew 5–7; Acts 2:42, 46) and "Kingdom Doings" (see Matthew 8–9; Acts 2:42-46). Each month, we spend three weeks learning, and then once a month we add one of the three fully relational "Kingdom Doing" rhythms.

Kingdom Teachings

1. **Learn**: Jesus taught and lived the gospel of his kingdom with those he invited along (Matthew 4:23; 9:35).

We will share our spiritual autobiographies or testimonies of how God has been working in our lives. These are a good starting place for learning and living the gospel because transparency and humility are the outcome.

We will follow the eight studies in this book to fuel disciple making conversations with those we invite along. After this, some form of a Discovery Bible Study is a helpful tool (see Appendix I).

Kingdom Doings

Once every month, our group does some sort of "Kingdom Doing" together. Each one is highly relational. Hence the rhythm: three weeks of Teachings, one week of Doing, three weeks of Teachings, one week of Doing, and so on.

2. **Serve**: Jesus served with those he invited along (John 13; Luke 22:27; See also Acts 2:43, 45).

3. **Eat**: Jesus ate and debriefed with those he invited along (Matthew 9:10–13; See also Acts 2:42, 46).

4. **Rest**: Jesus rested and Sabbathed with those he invited along (Matthew 26:36–46; See also Acts 2:42, 46).

This includes simply enjoying fellowship as well as time together in spiritual disciplines.

Five Steps to Start a Group

1. **Pray**

   - Pray and look (Colossians 4:2).
   - Pray that God will reveal two to four people in your life to join you in this journey of discipleship, and keep your eyes open for who God might be revealing to you.

2. **Invite**

   - Face-to-face, individual invitation (Matthew 4:19).
   - A simple but clear call to participate in a group following King Jesus.
   - Tell them why they stand out as someone whom you want to be in this group.

3. **Expectations**

   - Meet weekly – Come prepared.
   - Life-on-life format – Deepen relationships!
   - Life-changing accountability – Pray for each other, confess sins to each other, and hold each other accountable.
   - Time commitment – Accept that it will interfere with your life.
   - Multiplication – This isn't only for my transformation; it is also about becoming disciple makers.

4. **Covenant**

   - Look at the covenant in Appendix I.
   - Discuss and sign/affirm the group covenant. In some cases, it may be helpful to present the covenant at the first meeting and let each member discuss with their family before coming back to sign it.
   - Revisit the group covenant every quarter or when needed.

5. **Live It**

   - Start the group with personal autobiographies. Be vulnerable and transparent. Transformation happens in transparent community around the truth of God's word.
   - Practice weekly commitments together.
   - Curriculum:
     1) *Trust and Follow Jesus* by Bobby Harrington with Carl and Alicia Williamson
     2) Discovery Bible Study (begin with the Gospel of Mark)

"WHERE DO I START?"

First, prayerfully decide on an apprentice who will help you lead the group. Together, pray for God to help you find the two or three other people who should join your group. Ideally, there will be four or five total people per group.

"WHOM DO I LOOK FOR?"

- Ready to talk: non-Christians who are open to spiritual conversations.
- Ready to obey: pew-sitting believers who are ready to live out their faith even though it isn't easy.
- Ready to multiply: believers who want to make disciples who make disciples.
- F.A.T. people: Faithful, Available, and Teachable.

PRACTICALITIES

- Gender-specific groups.
- Ideally four or five people per group, multiply by a factor of two.
- Rotate who leads the discussion every week.
- Timespan will vary, but most groups will exist for nine to eighteen months (even two years) before multiplying.
- Stay connected after multiplying!

CHAPTER 1

God

Let's start the conversations with a story from the Bible. The story takes place around AD 50 in ancient Athens. It's about the apostle Paul, an early church leader, and it is recorded in the seventeenth chapter of the book of Acts (verses 16–31):

While Paul was waiting for them in Athens, he was greatly distressed to see that the city was full of idols. So, he reasoned in the synagogue with both Jews and God-fearing Greeks, as well as in the marketplace day by day with those who happened to be there. A group of Epicurean and Stoic philosophers began to debate with him. Some of them asked, "What is this babbler trying to say?" Others remarked, "He seems to be advocating foreign gods." They said this because Paul was preaching the good news about Jesus and the resurrection. Then they took him and brought him to a meeting of the Areopagus, where they said to him, "May we know what this new teaching is that you are presenting? You are bringing some strange ideas to our ears, and we would like to know what they mean." (All the Athenians and the foreigners who lived there spent their time doing nothing but talking about and listening to the latest ideas.)

Paul then stood up in the meeting of the Areopagus and said: "People of Athens! I see that in every way you are very religious. For as I walked around and looked carefully at your objects of worship, I even found an altar with this inscription: TO AN UNKNOWN GOD. So you are ignorant of the very thing you worship—and this is what I am going to proclaim to you.

"The God who made the world and everything in it is the Lord of heaven and earth and does not live in temples built by human hands. And he is not served by human hands, as if he needed anything. Rather, he himself gives everyone life and breath and everything else. From one man he made all the nations, that they should inhabit the whole earth; and he marked out their appointed times in history and the boundaries of their lands. God did this so that they would seek him and perhaps reach out for him and find him, though he is not far from any one of us. 'For in him we live and move and have our being.' As some of your own poets have said, 'We are his offspring.'

"Therefore, since we are God's offspring, we should not think that the divine being is like gold or silver or stone—an image made by human design and skill. In the past God overlooked such ignorance, but now he commands all people everywhere to repent. For he has set a day when he will judge the world with justice by the man he has appointed. He has given proof of this to everyone by raising him from the dead."

What was Paul's methodology for sharing his faith, and what was he preaching?

_____

_____

What is your reaction to the statement that God made you in the hope that you would personally seek him out, as described below?

> *God did this so that they would seek him and perhaps reach out for him and find him, though he is not far from any one of us.*

_____

_____

What steps do you need to take to seek God, to reach out for him, and to find him at a deeper level?

_____

_____

_____

_____

Our Awareness of God

When the apostle Paul talked to the people in Athens, he assumed a perspective about God. It is something that I have found to be true today—people intuitively and subconsciously know that God exists. I know that may sound naïve and unreasonable to some, especially to proclaimed atheists, who claim there is no God. But I have found that, after years of careful investigation, conversations, and personal experiences, even when studying with atheists in a graduate philosophy department, it is true.

Everyone intuitively senses that God exists.

I believe that most people will affirm, at a minimum, that a higher power is out there. This lines up with what the Bible teaches—that our intuitive consciousness of the created world itself somehow tells us God exists.

> For since the creation of the world God's invisible qualities—his eternal power and divine nature—have been clearly seen, being understood from what has been made, so that people are without excuse. (Romans 1:20)

This verse not only tells us that God exists but also that everyone intuitively *sees* God's eternal power and divine nature.

This discussion guide doesn't have the space to delve into the arguments for God's existence, though that is a beneficial endeavor (see Appendix II for a short summary of the three classic arguments). Instead, we will operate under the assumption that you, the reader, believe in God, but also that you may need help determining if the God revealed by Jesus is the true God and Creator of the world. Or maybe you just need help in understanding, trusting, and following Jesus.

The Value of Reasoning

As you may have already noticed in Acts 17, Paul "reasoned in the synagogue with the Jews and the devout persons . . . with those who happened to be there" (Acts 17:17, ESV). The Bible tells us that Jesus was once asked about how to inherit eternal life. As you read Jesus' answer, ask yourself: How does this apply to me?

> On one occasion an expert in the law stood up to test Jesus. "Teacher," he asked, "what must I do to inherit eternal life?" "What is written in the Law?" he replied. "How do you read it?" He answered, "'Love the Lord your God with all your heart and with all your soul and with

all your strength and with all your mind'; and, 'Love your neighbor as yourself.'" "You have answered correctly," Jesus replied. "Do this and you will live." (Luke 10:25–28)

We often think that love is a feeling, but in this passage, Jesus tells us that love is holistic, involving heart, soul, strength, and mind. Reflect on those four aspects of how you can express love for God. Fill in the blanks:

The easiest way for me to love God is with my _____ .

Why?

_____

_____

_____

_____

The hardest way for me to love God is with my _____ .

Why?

_____

_____

_____

_____

Explain in one sentence how you feel about approaching the Bible with an emphasis on the mind (reason).

_____

_____

_____

One of the things many people have a hard time with today is approaching the Bible with an emphasis on loving God with "the mind." Yet, if we seek a balanced approach to God, the mind will be an important part of how we love God holistically. All parts are important, so we don't want to neglect any aspect; we want all of them.

But, as a part of a holistic approach, the Bible tells us that the use of reason and factual thinking are important. They are necessary to properly love God. The Bible has an ancient proverb that helps us on this point.

Proverbs 24:3 describes the use of reason in a short but profound statement:

> By wisdom a house is built, and through understanding it is established.

How is it that wisdom and understanding are necessary to build the foundation of a house for a spiritual life?

_____

_____

Once the house's framework is established by wisdom, understanding, and reason, then other aspects of the house can be added.

The Three Elements of the Faith

There is one more thing to establish upfront as you build the foundation of a spiritual house for your life. People who have spent time studying the Bible say that they are constantly surprised by how simple and relevant its message is for our time. They point out that after a person spends the time to understand the teachings of Jesus in their original setting, then they usually find that Jesus is the most important source of meaning, hope, and direction in life.

But we want to help you by *keeping it simple* (without being simplistic).

So we are going to focus on the essential elements of the faith taught in scripture. People have found it helpful to summarize a specific way of looking at the various elements in the Bible. Think of concentric circles with core elements in the middle, and moving outward, the elements become more personal or relative.

Here is what we mean:

a. There are essential elements (or teachings) in the Bible that are *essential to your eternal destiny and standing with God.*
b. There are secondary elements in the Bible that are *important for your ongoing faithfulness to God and for living as God intended.*
c. There are third-level elements that God leaves for us to decide as *personal preferences or truths about which there is a lack of decisive evidence one way or the other.*[3]

This model and its three levels—understood as teachings and our faithfulness to these teachings—helps us make sense of the Bible. It also helps us prioritize certain teachings over others in the early phase of our journey as we explore biblical truth. Let me explain each level in more depth.

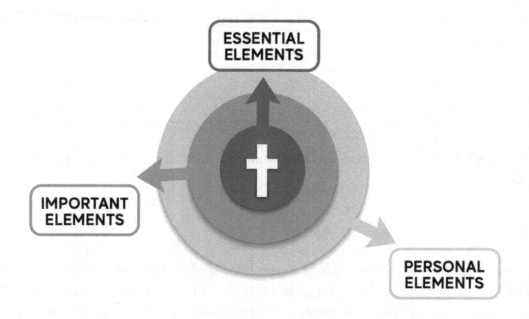

1. Essential Elements (sometimes called, "written in blood," or "first bucket teachings")

We believe the gospel we preach and the Jesus we display determines the kind of disciple a person becomes. The word "gospel" is not a common word today. It is the core of the Bible, and it simply means "the good news." Jesus Christ himself, especially his death and resurrection, is the "good news"—the best and most important announcement that anyone could ever hear.

The apostle Paul gives us a brief summary of the gospel in 1 Corinthians 15:3–7:

> For what I received I passed on to you as of first importance: that Christ died for our sins according to the Scriptures, that he was buried, that he was raised on the third day according to the Scriptures, and that he appeared to Cephas, and then to the Twelve. After that, he appeared to more than five hundred of the brothers and sisters at the same time, most of whom are still living, though some have fallen asleep. Then he appeared to James, then to all the apostles.

Some scholars summarize the essential elements of the faith by the "seven ones" found in Ephesians 4:4–7. Take a look at that summary:

> There is one **body** and one **Spirit**—just as you were called to the one **hope** that belongs to your call—one **Lord**, one **faith**, one **baptism**, one **God and Father of all**, who is over all and through all and in all. But grace was given to each of us according to the measure of Christ's gift. (Ephesians 4:4–7, ESV)

Dr. Scott Adair uses this text to create an easy-to-remember summary of the faith, using one's hands. We will describe it briefly below.

One Lord. Hold up your thumb and say, "Jesus Christ, the Son of God, is Lord."

ONE LORD

One God and Father of All. Point your index finger to the sky (as if to indicate "number one") and say, "There is one God, who is Father, Son, and Holy Spirit," Notice your index finger has three parts, and point to each one.

One Faith. Make the peace sign with index finger and middle finger. Trace the V as if descending into the grave, then rising again, as you say, "I believe in the death, the burial, and the resurrection of Jesus."

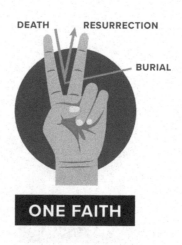

One Body. Point to the ring finger. This symbolizes the relational dimension of the Christian faith. The believer becomes part of the church, the bride of Christ, through faith in Jesus Christ.

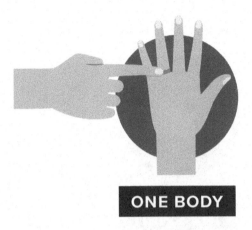

ONE BODY

One Baptism. Point to the pinky finger—the weak, short finger. This reminds us that we are weak and have sinned, and we need forgiveness. Baptism represents a tangible reference to the reality of sins being washed away (Acts 22:16).

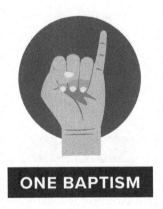

ONE BAPTISM

One Spirit. Open the whole hand with your palm pointed upward, as if to receive something from heaven. This gesture symbolizes the believer receiving the Holy Spirit, just as the Spirit came upon Jesus in baptism like a dove.

One Hope. Finally, raise your open hand to the sky, like you are asking a crowd of people to rise. This gesture reminds us of the promise of the resurrection of the dead.

The gospel is so simple that small children can understand it, and it is so profound that studies by the wisest theologians will never exhaust its riches.[4] This is the core of the Bible. It is that which calls us to make the decision to trust and follow Jesus.

2. Important Elements (sometimes called "written in ink" or "second bucket teachings")

When we are focused on the gospel and by faith adhere to the path of discipleship, we have a center point for our faith. This is the core teaching of the Bible. Other biblical truths, however, are also important to us because they come from God. These are the important elements. We seek to understand and live our lives in light of *all God's truth*. But we must be clear: our eternal destiny is not dependent on these secondary, yet important truths. People who completely trust in Jesus and have committed themselves to the path of discipleship often disagree on these important biblical teachings.

Important truths are things like how the local church should be structured (e.g., should it have a pastor or multiple elders; should they be male or female). It might also be something like whether or not a church truly practices active discipleship, or if they truly teach and help people to love and take care of one another. It could be how the church practices accountability (i.e., how should people be held accountable for the way they live their lives). Or it may be our understanding of predestination and free will.

We know that on many of these matters sincere Christians divide into different churches. Also, as individuals, sometimes our convictions about biblical truth at this level mean that we cannot "do church with other good Christians." We believe, as a general principle, that these issues do not destroy our salvation or make us "lost." Yes, these doctrinal differences are important, and we need to strive to be faithful in our understanding and practice of each one; yes, we must strive to believe and follow all of God's truth; yes, these matters have a big impact on the health of the local church and the health of our faith over the long term; and yes, we need to listen to one another and exhort one another to make sure that we are being faithful to God's truth in all things.

But no, we don't have to get everything just right to be saved. The gospel teaches us that we are all imperfect and struggling children who will *never get it all right* and who can only be saved by "grace through faith" (Ephesians 2:8–9). So we must often agree to disagree with our brothers and sisters and practice our faith differently. We are still united through our core faith in Jesus, but we often are not united in the same local church when this happens.

3. Personal Elements (sometimes called "written in pencil" or "third bucket teachings")

There is a third level of diversity among Christian people that we should also acknowledge. At this third level we can almost always stay together in a local church. We function together because we agree on the gospel and on the important—but secondary—elements of the faith. But on this third level of personal matters, where issues are less clear, God does not have a set path all of us must follow. Because the issue is relative or not clear, we agree to disagree. Some matters in the Bible are disputable, and some are very hard to understand. This compels us to adopt a stance where we respect honest, personal differences, while still being in close fellowship in the same church.

Here is an example of what I mean. While upholding that the Bible is the inspired and reliable Word of God, some Christians believe the days in Genesis 1 represent literal twenty-four-hour periods of time (that is, God created the world in six of these twenty-four-hour periods), and some Christians, with the same high view of Scripture, do not believe this view is accurate. How we understand personal truth is important in terms of our view of the authority of God's Word, but bright, godly, and sincere Christians have different understandings on something like how creation and evolution fit together. One's stance on this doctrine is a personal position; there are many questions, and there is a lot of ambiguity as a person comes to their best understanding. That's okay.

We might take something like having a glass of wine. Some Christians don't drink any alcohol, while other Christians do. The Bible teaches that it is wrong to get drunk (Ephesians 5:18), but that's the only clear line that can be drawn.

Therefore, we must be careful not to insist that our belief is the right one *for everyone else*. This is a matter of profound humility. These matters are grey—not black and white. We have great freedom of conscience to believe and practice what we personally think is God's best.

Again, in this book we are going to focus mostly upon the essential truths. It will involve understanding various important truths, but the essential ones will be central.

We want you to see this paradigm upfront so that it can help you to see the relative weight of various teachings in the Bible. We want to focus on the most central ones.

Practice speaking out loud the seven core doctrines found in Ephesians 4:4–7, and list them in the first category below under "Essential Elements." After that, make a list of important and personal elements to discuss with your group.

Essential elements:

_____

_____

Important elements:

_____

_____

Personal elements:

_____

_____

This book seeks to establish the key basics or elementary teachings of the faith (Hebrews 6:1–3; Ephesians 4:4–6). There are seven key concepts:

1. **Jesus in History.** Jesus was a real historical person, and most of the key elements of his life have been acknowledged and accepted by historians.
2. **Scripture.** God inspired the Bible and gave it to us for guidance.
3. **God's Holiness.** The Bible reveals that our core problem is sin, which separates us from a holy God. We must own it and repent of it by faith.
4. **God's Love.** Jesus demonstrated God's love when he came to rescue us by his crucifixion and enthronement as Lord and Messiah. We are to respond and place our faith in him.
5. **Lord and King.** True faith in Jesus means that we have a faithful faith that leads us to both trust and follow Jesus as our Lord and King.
6. **Commitment.** We make the commitment to turn to Jesus and place our faith in him through repentance, confession, and baptism.
7. **Discipleship.** We live as disciples (that is, followers of Jesus) by relying on God's Spirit and living out of faith with a local church.

For some people, these concepts are new. For others, they are the basics they have believed for years. Those who master this material will be the most effective at reaching other people who do not know Jesus and entering into a relationship where they can help them to trust and follow him. Repeating these studies helps create a DNA of discipleship and disciple makers in the church. A church culture that aligns with these teachings will be more effective at disciple making.

Which of the seven teachings described above are you most excited to dig into during the upcoming conversations (and why)?

_____

_____

_____

Group Discussion Questions

1. What principle can you identify from Paul's speech (to those in Athens) that helps you to better understand God?

2. Why are reason and the mind important in following Jesus, and what is one logical argument for God that is helpful for your believing in him?

3. How could memorizing the core doctrines in Ephesians 4, using the hand exercise, help you tell the story of God in a healthy way?

4. What is one area in which you need to be more obedient to God this week?

CHAPTER 2

Jesus in History

Key Theme: Jesus was a real historical person, and most of the key elements of his life have been acknowledged and accepted by historians.

We want to start with the question of historical truth. It's important for thinking people who approach the question of faith to be able to honestly ask, "Was Jesus a real person in history?" "Do we have good reason to believe that the things the Bible describes actually happened?" and, "What facts do we know, independent of the Bible, that show us whether or not the core things in the Bible about Jesus are true?"

1. Jesus is a historical figure. In fact, there is very good evidence for Jesus from *outside* the Bible. We can know, even today, that the things described in the Gospels have an objective basis in history.

Ancient non-Christian historians like Josephus and Tacitus record Jesus as a historical person. The popular archaeology journal *The Biblical Archaeology Review* asked the question, "Did Jesus Exist: Searching for Evidence Beyond the Bible?"[5] In this article, Lawrence Mykytiuk summarizes the evidence about Jesus from sources outside the Bible:

1. He existed as a man.
2. His personal name was Jesus.
3. He was called *Christos* in Greek, which is a translation of the Hebrew word *Messiah*.
4. He had a brother named James.
5. He won over both Jews and Greeks.
6. Jewish leaders of the day expressed unfavorable opinions about him.
7. Pilate rendered the decision that he should be executed.

8. His execution was specifically by crucifixion.

9. He was executed during Pontius Pilate's governorship over Judea (AD 26–36).

Why is it important to have historical evidence for Jesus from outside the Bible? Which point from the list is most surprising to you?

_____

_____

_____

_____

2. A leading expert on Jesus and his kingdom today is N. T. Wright, who summarizes the scholarly consensus about him among historians: "Jesus' life, his announcement of God's kingdom, his radical re-definition of that kingdom, and his death on a Roman cross—we can be certain of all that. Few serious historians of any background or belief would deny those facts."[6]

Why would it be important to know that these basic facts about Jesus are well-established and affirmed by the best historical scholars in the world today?

_____

_____

_____

3. The Bible teaches that those who believe in Jesus should have a healthy reverence for Christ and be able to give the reasons for their faith. Believers are to defend their convictions with gentleness and respect for non-believers.

> But in your hearts revere Christ as Lord. Always be prepared to give an answer to everyone who asks you to give the reason for the hope that you have. But do this with gentleness and respect. (1 Peter 3:15)

Why are gentleness and respect important when sharing one's faith?

_____

_____

_____

4. Our faith is not a blind faith but an informed faith. Our faith has good evidence and reason to back it up. For example, Luke wrote the Gospel of Luke to tell people about Jesus. But he wrote it only after searching the evidence.

> Many have undertaken to draw up an account of the things that have been fulfilled among us, just as they were handed down to us by those who from the first were eyewitnesses and servants of the word. With this in mind, since I myself have carefully investigated everything from the beginning, I too decided to write an orderly account for you, most excellent Theophilus, so that you may know the certainty of the things you have been taught. (Luke 1:1–4)

Why does having an informed faith matter, and why do you think Luke investigated for himself?

_____

_____

_____

5. Paul was an early believer in Jesus and a leader of the Christian faith. He explained to a Roman official named Festus what it meant to believe in Jesus. Paul was very intelligent, and Festus thought Paul might be insane to believe in Jesus. Paul reminded him of the historical evidence for Jesus as a reason for him to believe.

> At this point Festus interrupted Paul's defense. "You are out of your mind, Paul!" he shouted. "Your great learning is driving you insane." "I am not insane, most excellent Festus," Paul replied. "What I am saying is true and reasonable. The king is familiar with these things, and I can speak freely to him. I am convinced that none of this has escaped his notice, because it was not done in a corner. (Acts 26:24–26)

Have you ever considered someone else to be unreasonable or out of their mind for their faith? Why is it important to be grounded in what is true and reasonable?

_____

_____

_____

_____

6. The faith we follow is focused upon the resurrection of Jesus from the dead. The Bible teaches that the resurrection is a fundamental truth and that many witnesses attested to it. As you read the following passage, note both the importance of the resurrection and the apostle Paul's mention of eyewitnesses. Most of them were still living twenty-five years after the resurrection—and Paul was implying that the people in Corinth could (did) talk to them.

> For what I received I passed on to you as of first importance: that Christ died for our sins according to the Scriptures, that he was buried, that he was raised on the third day according to the Scriptures, and that he appeared to Cephas, and then to the Twelve. After that, he appeared to more than five hundred of the brothers and sisters at the same time, most of whom are still living, though some have fallen asleep [died]. (1 Corinthians 15:3–6)

What would your reaction be if you could talk to eyewitnesses of Jesus' resurrection today—just like these people were able to do then?

_____

_____

_____

Summary

Atheists and leaders from other religions (like Judaism, Buddhism, and Islam) have proposed alternative theories to the resurrection. Scholars have investigated them all, and none have been found to be a good alternative explanation. No theory makes as much sense as the reality of the resurrection.[7]

You can read three articles that I (Bobby) have written on the historical evidence for Jesus Christ and the resurrection at Renew.org. Read the article on the resurrection (see the QR code to the right), and then if you have time, you might check out the other two articles (see links within the article).

The eyewitnesses of the resurrection were closest to the facts. They truly believed it. We know from history that their beliefs were so strong that they did not just claim that Jesus rose from the dead; they radically altered their lives, lived through awful persecution, and died terrible deaths as martyrs rather than giving up their faith in the resurrection. The earliest eyewitnesses bet their lives that Jesus' resurrection pointed to a better life after death.

The resurrection of Jesus is also the best explanation for the start of Christianity and the early church. Something caused the explosion of this new religion into the world. It started in Jerusalem, where the evidence for the resurrection was best known, and it spread to the outer reaches of the Roman Empire.

The evidence for Jesus and his resurrection is strong. Those with faith should also know that the evidence provides factual support for what they believe in their hearts—that the Bible accurately reflects the historical truth about Jesus.

Have you ever altered your life because of a conviction based on objective evidence? Why is this so powerful?

_____

_____

_____

Group Discussion Questions

1. In your own words, how would you talk about Jesus as a historical person?
2. Why is the resurrection a fundamental truth, and what place could it have in a conversation about "hope" for you? Explain.
3. What is the significance of eyewitness accounts?
4. Who are a few people with whom you will share the insights from this book and/or share your faith this week?

CHAPTER 3

Scripture

Key Theme: God inspired the Bible and gave it to us for our guidance.

Once we know that Jesus existed and that there are good reasons to consider the Gospel accounts about him to contain accurate information, we're ready for the next step. In this section, we want to look at what Jesus claimed about his teachings.

Again, we are on solid ground to assume based upon historical evidence that the Gospels accurately present Jesus. That's because in everything we can look at objectively in history, we find that the Gospels are accurate. So we are going to assume the continued accuracy of the accounts as we look at what Jesus said about his teachings.

The written records of Jesus' teachings are important. Especially if Jesus expected his apostles and followers to carry on his teachings and to make other followers (disciples), it was necessary to write them down. These teachings became part of the Bible.

Before we look at these teachings, it is helpful to understand how people looked at Scripture in Jesus' time. Knowing this will help us to determine how Jesus' teachings would have been understood and preserved for us.

Scripture in Jesus' Time

Contrary to what most people think, everyday people in Jesus' time were typically literate. Historians have learned that first-century Jewish people had tremendous respect for Scripture. They believed God had commanded them to teach the Old Testament writings (the first part of the Bible) to their children, *so children were required to learn to read and write.* Josephus was a historian living at that time, and he wrote about Jewish people and their children. He said that God's law "orders that [children] shall be taught to read and shall learn both the laws and the deeds of their forefathers."[8] This meant that the average Jewish person at that time could read. So, even though Jesus lived two thousand years ago, both Jesus and the people of his time regularly discussed the meaning of the Scriptures (this reality is reflected in the Gospels in the New Testament).

Jewish people not only read widely, but they also made sure the Scriptures were accurately passed down. The Old Testament is the record of God and the Jewish people from the time of Moses (from the mid-1400s BC to 1260 BC) up until the last books of the Old Testament (around 400–165 BC). Recent discoveries like the Dead Sea Scrolls at Qumran in Israel show us how careful the people were to preserve the teachings of the Old Testament. The people at Qumran lived before and during the time of Jesus, and they would check every small part of Scripture to make sure it was accurately copied; then, they would check and re-check it. They were accurate and neat in all their copying work, as my picture of a scroll of Isaiah from 150 BC below shows. Notice the clear and neat freehand writing.

They would even take ritualistic baths after their work to ensure that their work was consecrated to God and that they were faithful scribes, accurately copying God's words.

It's also important to know that the people in the time of Jesus widely relied upon the educational method of memorization. Jewish boys had an established practice of reading and memorizing portions of the Old Testament starting at five or six years of age.[9] Some teachers even had the entire Old Testament committed to memory.

It was their practice to memorize important teachings—the Scriptures and the teachings in the synagogue. There is an entire Jewish tradition (the oral interpretation of the Law by leading rabbis in the time of Jesus) that was very active in the time of Jesus. These teachings were passed on for hundreds of years and were only written down around 200 BC. The important teachings of their leaders were memorized and carefully passed down from generation to generation. That is what they did to ensure accurate record keeping.

I say this to point out that when Jesus gave his teachings, he gave them to people who were trained to write down and memorize the teachings of their rabbis (religious leaders). As a well-known teacher, Jesus' teaching would have been immediately written down and memorized by his disciples.

Furthermore, many parts of Jesus' teachings were structured so that they could be easily memorized. Take the Sermon on the Mount, Jesus' most famous teaching on moral issues, as a case in point (Matthew 5–7). It was structured like the teaching of philosophers in the Roman world, whose teachings were summarized in a form that was easily memorized. From the sayings at the beginning of the Sermon on the Mount, to the introduction proper (Matthew 5:17–20), to the first six contrasted teachings, through to the conclusion (Matthew 7:20–28), the structure was designed to make it easy to memorize.

The Jewish practice of preserving teachings intact like those found in the Gospels would have been commonplace. From the earliest times, the memories of Jesus' life and teaching would have been considered sacred and been memorized and written down.[10] In this way, the earliest disciples would have naturally ensured that Jesus' words and deeds were accurately established. This perspective is a key to understanding the development of the Christian Scriptures.

We will focus on Jesus and his teachings through the creation of the Gospels and the rest of the New Testament scriptures in this chapter. Those who have questions about which books should be considered Scripture and the reliability of the manuscripts will find the material by scholars Craig Blomberg and Michael Kroger to be helpful, along with information that can be found at Renew.org.[11]

1. How do these historical facts help us when it comes to the question of whether there could have been good written records of Jesus' teachings?

_____

_____

_____

2. Jesus promised that God was with his disciples, ensuring that they had an accurate recounting of what Jesus said and did. God promised that the Holy Spirit (God's invisible presence) would guide the apostles and help them to remember everything to make sure it was recorded accurately. Notice the promise:

> These words you hear are not my own; they belong to the Father who sent me. All this I have spoken while still with you. But the Advocate, the Holy Spirit, whom the Father will send in my name, will teach you all things and will remind you of everything I have said to you. (John 14:24b–26)

In what way does this passage give us additional perspective on how the apostles could accurately record Jesus' teachings?

_____

_____

_____

3. Jesus said that people should believe in him, but even more, he said that he spoke for God. God, Jesus said, would use Jesus' words as the basis for our judgment at the end of time:

> If anyone hears my words but does not keep them, I do not judge that person. For I did not come to judge the world, but to save the world. There is a judge for the one who rejects me and does not accept my words; the very words I have spoken will condemn them at the last day. For I did not speak on my own, but the Father who sent me commanded me to say all that I have spoken. (John 12:47–49)

According to this passage, who gave Jesus his words and how will Jesus' words be used on the final day of judgment?

_____

_____

_____

4. Jesus acknowledges that many people call him "Lord," which is a word that means "master and God." According to Jesus, saying he is "Lord," is only meaningful if we hear his words and put them into practice.

> Why do you call me, "Lord, Lord," and do not do what I say? As for everyone who comes to me and hears my words and puts them into practice, I will show you what they are like. They are like a man building a house, who dug down deep and laid the foundation on rock. When a flood came, the torrent struck that house but could not shake it, because it was well built. But the one who hears my words and does not put them into practice is like a man who built a house on the ground without a foundation. The moment the torrent struck that house, it collapsed, and its destruction was complete. (Luke 6:46–49)

How can it be that if we hear and put Jesus' words into practice it is like building a house with a good foundation?

_____

_____

_____

5. Jesus committed his teachings to the apostles. He then gave them the job of teaching people to obey everything Jesus taught.

> Then Jesus came to them and said, "All authority in heaven and on earth has been given to me. Therefore go and make disciples of all nations, baptizing them in the name of the Father and of the Son and of the Holy Spirit, and teaching them to obey everything

I have commanded you. And surely I am with you always, to the very end of the age."
(Matthew 28:18–20)

Does Jesus teach us to learn everything he commanded or to obey everything he commanded—and what is the difference?

_____

_____

_____

6. Paul was an apostle of Jesus, and he taught people that Scripture is our inspired guide.

All Scripture is God-breathed and is useful for teaching, rebuking, correcting and training in righteousness, so that the servant of God may be thoroughly equipped for every good work.
(2 Timothy 3:16–17)

Which of the four purposes of Scripture described in this passage is the most difficult use of Scripture to apply to yourself today?

_____

_____

_____

7. Paul proceeded, in the verses after 2 Timothy 3:17, to describe the presence of God and Jesus under the banner of "the Word," meaning that the teaching of Jesus through the apostles is very much "Jesus' Word."

In the presence of God and of Christ Jesus, who will judge the living and the dead, and in view of his appearing and his kingdom, I give you this charge. Preach the word; be prepared in season and out of season; correct, rebuke and encourage—with great patience and careful instruction. For the time will come when people will not put up with sound doctrine.

> Instead, to suit their own desires, they will gather around them a great number of teachers to say what their itching ears want to hear. (2 Timothy 4:1–4)

What happens to make us gravitate to teachers who say what "our itching ears want to hear," and how do you envision stopping yourself from doing that?

_____

_____

_____

8. We believe, based upon history, that the Bible contains accurate teachings. The Bible also says that God guided the process of creating prophecies in Scripture.

> We also have the prophetic message as something completely reliable, and you will do well to pay attention to it, as to a light shining in a dark place, until the day dawns and the morning star rises in your hearts. Above all, you must understand that no prophecy of Scripture came about by the prophet's own interpretation of things. For prophecy never had its origin in the human will, but prophets, though human, spoke from God as they were carried along by the Holy Spirit. (2 Peter 1:19–21)

What do you think it means that people were "carried along by the Holy Spirit" to write what they did and, again, how does that give people extra confidence in the teachings of Scripture?

_____

_____

_____

9. The following passage is a very important guide for us in our day. It describes the people of Berea (a town in the ancient world) as being noble. They were noble because they examined the

Scriptures to see if what was being taught was true. We want to be noble in the same way that they were noble.

> As soon as it was night, the believers sent Paul and Silas away to Berea. On arriving there, they went to the Jewish synagogue. Now the Berean Jews were of more noble character than those in Thessalonica, for they received the message with great eagerness and examined the Scriptures every day to see if what Paul said was true. As a result, many of them believed, as did also a number of prominent Greek women and many Greek men. (Acts 17:10–12)

What are your habits with studying Scripture? What has worked well for you, and is there anything you want to try differently?

_____

_____

_____

Group Discussion Questions

1. In your own words, how would you talk about Scripture and how it was passed down?
2. How do Scripture and obedience fit together?
3. What role does the Holy Spirit play in Scripture?
4. What is a passage of Scripture that has recently impacted your faith that you can share with the group?

CHAPTER 4

God Is Holy

Key Theme: The Bible shows that because God is holy, our core problem is our sin, which separates us from God. We must own our sin and repent of it by faith.

Now that we know how Scripture came to us and the good reasons to believe it was reliably guided by God, we are ready to look at the core problem that exists between human beings and God. It begins with an understanding of what it means for God to be holy.

When we describe God as "holy," it means God is "pure, free from every stain, wholly perfect and immaculate in every detail."[12] To say God is holy means no sin, wrongdoing, evil, or anything bad exists in him. "God is light; in him there is no darkness at all," the Bible says (1 John 1:5).

God's holiness explains why human beings are separated from God and destined to face punishment if they are not rescued. The good news is that God, ever since the time of Adam and Eve, has run after sinful humanity. Immediately after Adam and Eve ate the forbidden fruit, God shows up in the garden. God is right in the midst of the Cain and Able story, even pleading with Cain, "Sin is crouching at the door. Its desire is contrary to you, but you must rule over it" (Genesis 4:7b, ESV). Every time we sin, that sin begins to control us, shackle us, and rule over us.[13]

The creation story is a model of the entire human race, not solely Adam and Eve. It tells us what's wrong with humanity. We cannot handle the pull of sin, selfishness, and evil our ancestors brought into the human experience by choosing to eat from the Tree of Knowledge of Good and Evil.

The shackles of sin separate us from God, but the gospel is that God sent Jesus to die so that our separation would be eradicated.

> There is therefore now no condemnation for those who are in Christ Jesus. For the law of the Spirit of life has set you free in Christ Jesus from the law of sin and death. For God has done

what the law, weakened by the flesh, could not do. By sending his own Son in the likeness of sinful flesh and for sin, he condemned sin in the flesh, in order that the righteous requirement of the law might be fulfilled in us, who walk not according to the flesh but according to the Spirit. (Romans 8:1–4, ESV)

The Bible teaches that God made Adam and Eve, the first humans, to live in an innocent state in the garden of Eden. But they also had an enemy. Satan was there, as a snake, to tempt Adam and Eve to sin and turn away from God, to which they succumbed. Now, we are all separated from God, gravitating to sin and living life without trusting and following him.

1. When God created humans in the garden of Eden, he wanted to keep them from the autonomous knowledge of good and evil. It was necessary to establish a boundary. Influenced by Satan (as a snake), Adam and Eve disobeyed.

And the LORD God commanded the man, "You are free to eat from any tree in the garden; but you must not eat from the tree of the knowledge of good and evil, for when you eat of it you will surely die." (Genesis 2:16–17)

The serpent was the shrewdest of all the wild animals the LORD God had made. One day he asked the woman, "Did God really say you must not eat the fruit from any of the trees in the garden?" "Of course we may eat fruit from the trees in the garden," the woman replied. "It's only the fruit from the tree in the middle of the garden that we are not allowed to eat. God said, 'You must not eat it or even touch it; if you do, you will die.'" "You won't die!" the serpent replied to the woman. "God knows that your eyes will be opened as soon as you eat it, and you will be like God, knowing both good and evil." (Genesis 3:1–5, NLT)

The woman was convinced. She saw that the tree was beautiful, and its fruit looked delicious, and she wanted the wisdom it would give her. So she took some of the fruit and ate it. Then she gave some to her husband, who was with her, and he ate it, too. At that moment their eyes were opened, and they suddenly felt shame at their nakedness. So they sewed fig leaves together to cover themselves. When the cool evening breezes were blowing, the man and his wife heard the LORD God walking about in the garden. So they hid from the LORD God among the trees. Then the LORD God called to the man, "Where are you?" He replied, "I heard you walking in the garden, so I hid. I was afraid because I was naked." (Genesis 3:6–10, NLT)

Then the LORD God said, "Look, the human beings have become like us, knowing both good and evil. What if they reach out, take fruit from the tree of life, and eat it? Then they will live forever!" So the LORD God banished them from the Garden of Eden, and he sent Adam out to cultivate the ground from which he had been made. (Genesis 3:22–23, NLT)

How did Adam and Eve sin? How did God ensure that Adam and Eve would eventually die?

_____

_____

_____

2. When Adam and Eve sinned, God said that they would die. The following passage describes the state of humanity after Adam and Eve's fall into sin.

As for you, you were dead in your transgressions and sins, in which you used to live when you followed the ways of this world and of the ruler of the kingdom of the air, the spirit who is now at work in those who are disobedient. All of us also lived among them at one time, gratifying the cravings of our sinful nature and following its desires and thoughts. Like the rest, we were by nature objects of wrath. (Ephesians 2:1–4)

In what ways does Satan influence the world? How does he influence you?

_____

_____

_____

3. Many of us do not know what is sinful in God's eyes.

The acts of the flesh are obvious: sexual immorality, impurity and debauchery; idolatry and witchcraft; hatred, discord, jealousy, fits of rage, selfish ambition, dissensions, factions and envy; drunkenness, orgies, and the like. I warn you, as I did before, that those who live like this will not inherit the kingdom of God. (Galatians 5:19–21)

We must accept what God calls sin and not let the world define right and wrong for us. As you review that list, notice how it ends with a sober warning: _those who live in these ways will not inherit_

God's eternal kingdom! Look at each item in the list below again and mark those you are currently struggling with:

- *Sexual immorality* = any sexual activity except between a male and a female in marriage. This means that sex before marriage, sex outside of marriage, and homosexual sexual unions are sinful (Romans 1:26–27).
- *Impurity and debauchery* = a wild, party lifestyle
- *Idolatry* = worshipping other gods like money, success, and admiration from others
- *Witchcraft* (*pharmakeia* in Greek) = drugs, spells, contacting the dead
- *Hatred, discord* = bitterness and strife
- *Jealousy* = bad attitudes because you want for yourself what others have
- *Fits of rage* = angry outbursts, uncontrolled episodes
- *Selfish ambition* = focused concern about yourself to the exclusion of others
- *Dissensions, factions* = divisiveness and causing trouble between people
- *Envy* = a bad attitude toward people because you want what they have
- *Drunkenness* = getting intoxicated with alcohol, getting intoxicated with marijuana
- *Orgies* = partying and involvement with promiscuous sex
- *And the like* = other things that reflect selfish sin . . .

Write out a prayer to God that confesses your sins:

_____

_____

_____

4. Humans, by nature, are separated from God because of our sin, and we need God to save us because we cannot save ourselves from brokenness.

> Your iniquities have separated you from your God; your sins have hidden his face from you, so that he will not hear. (Isaiah 59:2)

a. Sin separates us from God.

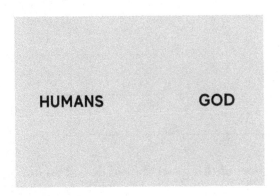

God — He is holy, and he is love.

Humans — God made humans in his image, but we do sinful, wrong things.

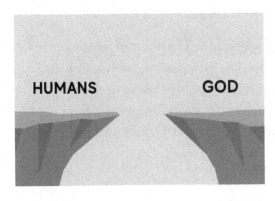

God and Humans – We are separated because God is holy and humans act out of their sinful nature.

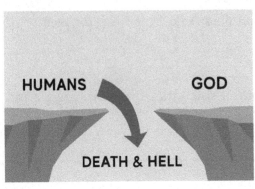

Human Deeds — We are lost (to death and hell) and separated from God because of our sin. Only God can take away our sin. Unless God saves us, we are lost.

b. In order for a human to have a relationship with God, the wall must be broken down and sin must be forgiven.

> As the Scriptures say, "No one is good—not even one. No one has real understanding; no one is seeking God. All have turned away from God; all have gone wrong. No one does good, not even one." (Romans 3:10–12)

Go back through the passages in this lesson, and reflect on your sins. Write down your thoughts about a God who comes down to earth to rescue you.

_____

_____

_____

5. Sin often involves the affections of our hearts or the neglect of things we should do but do not.

The sins of the heart are described in 2 Timothy 3:1–5. Notice how this can include religious people.

> But mark this: There will be terrible times in the last days. People will be lovers of themselves, lovers of money, boastful, proud, abusive, disobedient to their parents, ungrateful, unholy, without love, unforgiving, slanderous, without self-control, brutal, not lovers of the good, treacherous, rash, conceited, lovers of pleasure rather than lovers of God—having a form of godliness but denying its power. Have nothing to do with such people. (2 Timothy 3:1–5)

Sins of neglect are described in James 4:17:

> If anyone, then, knows the good they ought to do and doesn't do it, it is sin for them. (James 4:17)

Consider the list of sins from 2 Timothy. Identify two to three sins with which you struggle and one specific action that you want to take to begin changing.

_____

_____

_____

6. There is good news—God loves us and wants to forgive us of our sin. He wants us to trust him and follow him so that our sins can be forgiven. We do this by faith as we believe what God says in the Bible about sin. Repentance is a change in the way we feel and think that leads to a change in what we do.

- Sin is powerful. It easily entangles our lives.
- Sin is pleasurable; that's why we sin.
- Sin is deceitful.
- Sin is my responsibility: I cannot blame others for my sin because I am accountable for my life.
- We can overcome sin with the help of Jesus Christ and the power of his Spirit.

> Godly sorrow brings repentance that leads to salvation and leaves no regret, but worldly sorrow brings death. See what this godly sorrow has produced in you: what earnestness, what eagerness to clear yourselves, what indignation, what alarm, what longing, what concern, what readiness to see justice done. At every point you have proved yourselves to be innocent in this matter. (2 Corinthians 7:10–11)

What would it look like if your faith in Jesus led you to repent the way this passage describes?

_____

_____

_____

7. Repentance is important because we will all be raised up and will stand before God for a final judgment of our lives. We want to repent before our lives end, when we'll give an account of our sinful actions to God. Those who do not repent and put their faith in Jesus will go to hell.

> For we must all appear before the judgment seat of Christ, so that each of us may receive what is due us for the things done while in the body, whether good or bad. (2 Corinthians 5:10)

> And if your foot causes you to stumble, cut it off. It is better for you to enter life crippled than to have two feet and be thrown into hell. And if your eye causes you to stumble, pluck it out. It is better for you to enter the kingdom of God with one eye than to have two eyes and be thrown into hell, where "the worms that eat them do not die, and the fire is not quenched." (Mark 9:46–48)

What specific steps do you need to take to ensure that you are living a life that seeks faithfulness to God?

_____

_____

_____

Group Discussion Questions

1. What does it mean for God to be holy, and how does it affect our relationship with him?
2. What are stories from the Bible about sin and how God reacts to sin?
3. What does it look like to live according to the Spirit and not the flesh?
4. How can you apply this lesson to your life this week?

CHAPTER 5

God Is Love

Key Theme: Jesus showed God's love when he came to rescue us by dying on the cross and rising from the dead. We are to respond and place our faith in him.

In the last chapter, we focused on God's holiness. We are now ready to focus on God's love. It's only in the light of God's holiness that God's love can truly be seen. This is why John 3:16 would win, hands-down, in a contest to discover the most known and loved verse of Scripture:

> For God so loved the world that he gave his one and only Son, that whoever believes in him shall not perish but have eternal life. (John 3:16)

God did not want human beings to be cut off from him because of his holiness, so in his love, God found a way to take away human sin. In Jesus, God entered into our world to die for us and save us through costly, sacrificial love.

> For God did not send his Son into the world to condemn the world, but to save the world through him. (John 3:17–18)

> But God demonstrates his own love for us in this: While we were still sinners, Christ died for us. (Romans 5:8)

Let's look at a list of important contrasts. This short list helps us to understand how God is different than people presume. Our natural inclination is to think that as sinful people, we must approach God, earn our way, make sacrifices, and suffer for God. We think that if we do this, then somehow God might accept us. This concept is at the heart of all false religious beliefs. The Bible reveals a different kind of God.

Natural Human Thought	Biblical Teaching
Humanity approaches God.	God approaches humanity.
Humans suffer for God.	God suffers for humanity.
God receives human gifts.	God gives his own Son.
Sinners reconcile themselves to God.	God reconciles sinners.

Jesus' Life, Death, and Resurrection

The Bible records how Jesus came into the world, lived, and taught us God's ways. In Chapter 2, we presented a brief overview of Jesus' life—from his birth in Bethlehem to his death and resurrection in Jerusalem. It's important to remember Jesus' whole life, not just his birth, the cross, and the resurrection.

Jesus did many good things. He lived as our role model and an ideal human. He healed people, cast out demons, and came as humanity's teacher. Luke records the apostle Peter's summary of Jesus' life in these words:

> You know the message God sent to the people of Israel, announcing the good news of peace through Jesus Christ, who is Lord of all. You know what has happened throughout the province of Judea, beginning in Galilee after the baptism that John preached—how God anointed Jesus of Nazareth with the Holy Spirit and power, and how he went around doing good and healing all who were under the power of the devil, because God was with him. We are witnesses of everything he did in the country of the Jews and in Jerusalem. (Acts 10:36–39)

All of these things are part of the gospel, the good news about Jesus. We will look at Jesus' kingdom and teaching and what it means to be his disciple in an upcoming chapter, but for our purposes here, we want to focus on what Peter described next and how Jesus came to save us. He died and rose again, and he provides us with the forgiveness of sins.

> They killed him by hanging him on a cross, but God raised him from the dead on the third day and caused him to be seen. He was not seen by all the people, but by witnesses whom God had already chosen—by us who ate and drank with him after he rose from the dead. He commanded us to preach to the people and to testify that he is the one whom God appointed as judge of the living and the dead. All the prophets testify about him that everyone who believes in him receives forgiveness of sins through his name. (Acts 10:39–43)

Here is a summary of Jesus' life:

Jesus came as this Messiah, our King, and in him, the kingdom of God broke into this sinful world. Jesus came to reveal the true nature of God and to restore and redeem God's original intent for humanity. Jesus' mission led him to the cross, where he suffered and died to save all people, both the Jews and the Gentiles (those not physically descended from Abraham). After three days, Jesus rose from the dead, freeing us from Satan; then, he ascended into heaven. He is coming back again to fully restore God's kingdom. By repentance and faith in Jesus and his finished work on the cross, we can enter into his kingdom. He takes away our sin and gives us the gift of the Holy Spirit, and we are adopted into his Father's family. Our old identity is dead, and we are a new creation through the grace of God by faith in Jesus and what Jesus has done for us. We now live a new life, trusting and following him as his disciples.

1. We live between Jesus' first coming—when he died for our sins, was raised from the dead, and ascended into heaven—and his second coming, when he will return to judge the living and the dead and establish his eternal kingdom.

In 1 Corinthians 15:1–6 as the apostle Paul prepares to give us the gospel in summary form, he highlights several of the benefits of the gospel for us:

> Now I would remind you, brothers, of the gospel I preached to you, which you received, in which you stand, and by which you are being saved, if you hold fast to the word I preached to you—unless you believed in vain. For I delivered to you as of first importance what I also received. (1 Corinthians 15:1–3a, ESV)

Paul's language is clear: believing, receiving, and standing in the gospel that has been preached to us saves us! Jesus and his work on the cross are the basis of our standing with God, and there is nothing more important! The passage goes on to summarize the core events of the gospel announcement:

> . . . that Christ died for our sins in accordance with the scriptures, that he was buried, that he was raised on the third day in accordance with the scriptures, and that he appeared to Cephas, then to the twelve. Then he appeared to more than five hundred brothers at one time, most of whom are still alive, though some have fallen asleep. (1 Corinthians 15:3–6, ESV)

Why is the gospel the ultimate good news?

_____

_____

_____

2. The Atonement. The word "atonement" means "at-one-ment," and it is a word that describes how Jesus makes us at one with God.

Look at the following passages, which describe Jesus' atonement for us:

> [Christ] is the atoning sacrifice for our sins, and not only for ours but also for the sins of the whole world. (1 John 2:2)

> For God was in Christ, reconciling the world to himself, no longer counting people's sins against them. This is the wonderful message he has given us to tell others . . . "Be reconciled to God!" For God made Christ, who never sinned, to be the offering for our sin, so that we could be made right with God through Christ. (2 Corinthians 5:19–21, NLT)

> We are made right in God's sight when we trust in Jesus Christ to take away our sins. And we all can be saved in this same way, no matter who we are or what we have done. For all have sinned; all fall short of God's glorious standard. Yet now God in his gracious kindness declares us not guilty. He has done this through Christ Jesus, who has freed us by taking away our sins. For God sent Jesus to take the punishment for our sins and to satisfy God's anger against us. We are made right with God when we believe that Jesus shed his blood, sacrificing his life for us. (Romans 3:22–25, NLT)

How does Jesus provide for us so that we can experience atonement with God?

_____

_____

_____

3. Grace. This is the unearned gift of a right standing with God. It is his posture toward sinful people, which has been revealed in Jesus. In grace, God gives us the free gift of Jesus, whose life, death, and resurrection establish our right standing with God and save us from the eternal consequences of sin. By grace, we are free to receive God's offer of forgiveness and place our faith in Jesus.

Faith is more than a mere intellectual agreement with facts or a warm heart toward Jesus that is not faithful to him otherwise. It is both *trust and commitment to follow*. It is allegiance, loyalty, and faithfulness to Jesus: who he is, what he teaches, and what he has done for us. The Bible describes what this "by-grace-through-faith" salvation is.

> For by grace you have been saved, through faith—and this not from yourselves, it is the gift of God—not by works, so that no one can boast. For we are God's handiwork, created in Christ Jesus to do good works, which God prepared in advance for us to do. (Ephesians 2:8–10)

A. T. Robertson, an expert on New Testament Greek, describes it succinctly: "Grace is God's part, faith ours."[14]

What does "grace" look like in your life?

_____

_____

How is "faith" active in your life?

_____

_____

4. Justice. To be "just" is to give the proper penalty for wrongdoing (or reward for doing right). The human mind will often ask, "How can a loving God send people to hell?" The Bible wants us to answer the deeper question: "How can a holy God not send everyone to hell?" Rephrased, this question is, "How can a holy God save us?"[15] The holiness and love of God came together in the sacrifice of Jesus on the cross.

The Bible scholar C. B. Cranfield puts it this way:

> For God simply to pass over sins would be altogether incompatible with his righteousness. He would not be the good and merciful God had he been content to pass over sins indefinitely, for this would have been to condone evil—a denial of his own nature and a cruel betrayal of sinners. God has in fact been able to hold his hand and pass over sins, without compromising his goodness and mercy, because his intention has all along been to deal with them once and for all, decisively and finally, through the Cross.[16]

How does Jesus' sacrifice help us to understand both God's holiness and love?

_____

_____

_____

5. God's Forgiveness. We are saved by grace through faith, and this is both an event (our justification) and a process in which we learn to become more and more faithful (our sanctification). In other words, it continues from the time of our conversion through the end of our lives.

In the Bible, the word "walk" is a common metaphor for the basic direction of one's life. So a person with faith in Jesus "walks in the way of Jesus" or "walks in the light." One of the most helpful passages for dealing with sin in terms of walking is 1 John 1:5b–9:

> God is light; in him there is no darkness at all. If we claim to have fellowship with him and yet walk in darkness, we lie and do not live out the truth. But if we walk in the light, as he is in the light, we have fellowship with one another, and the blood of Jesus, his Son, purifies us from all sin. If we claim to be without sin, we deceive ourselves and the truth is not in us. If we confess our sins, he is faithful and just and will forgive us our sins and purify us from all unrighteousness. (ESV)

> By this we may know that we are in him: whoever says he abides in him ought to walk in the same way in which he walked. (1 John 2:5b–6, ESV)

When we stumble and fall into sin, as we seek to follow Jesus, what does this passage teach us to do to find ongoing forgiveness with God?

_____

_____

_____

Please review the diagrams on the next page as a reminder of what it means to make the commitment to trust and follow Jesus.

How Faith in Jesus Renews Our Relationship with God

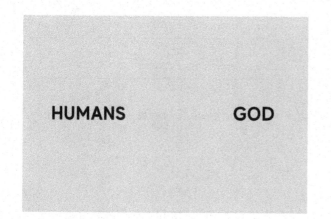

God — He is holy, and he is love.

Humans — God made humans in his image, but we do sinful, wrong things.

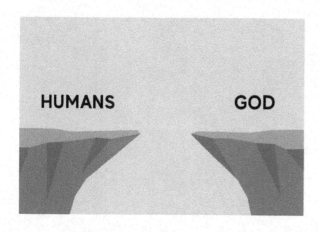

God and Humans — We are separated because God is holy and humans sin, acting out of their sinful nature.

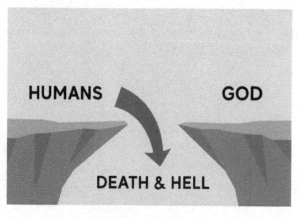

Human Deeds — We are lost (to death and hell) because of our sin—and all good deeds and attempts to make ourselves right with God fail. Only God can take away our sin. Unless God saves us, we are lost.

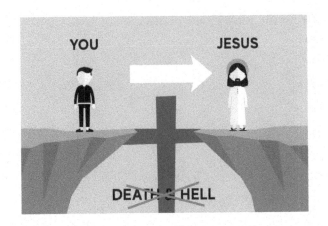

Jesus Christ — God so loved humanity that he sent Jesus Christ into the world to save us. Jesus showed the way by his teachings and life, and he paid for all our sins when he died on the cross and rose from the dead, and he is enthroned as Lord and King. He makes a bridge for us and offers us the way to get right with God.

Faith — We must personally respond and place our faith in Jesus if we want to be right with God. This commitment of faith means we will turn from sinful lifestyles and trust and follow Jesus. We express this commitment to place our faith in Jesus by a verbal confession and water baptism.

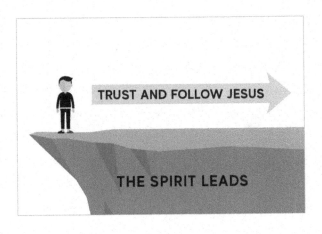

Trust and Follow Jesus (Faith) — We live new lives where we trust and follow Jesus, as the Spirit leads, as disciples. A disciple follows Jesus, is changed by Jesus, and is committed to the mission of Jesus.

Group Discussion Questions

1. How would you share God's story and/or how you've seen God's love in your story?
2. What are some ways that Jesus lived as our role model and the ideal human?
3. How does our culture's view of Christianity differ from the Bible's view of disciples of Jesus?
4. How would you draw the gospel in pictures?

CHAPTER 6

Lord and King

Key Theme: True faith in Jesus means we have a faithful faith—that we both trust and follow Jesus as his disciples, surrendering to him as our Lord and King.

When Jesus came into the world, he came as God's promised Messiah to establish God's long-promised kingdom. The kingdom is both "the reign" of God and "the realm" in which God reigns.[17] Jesus established the kingdom of God by his life and ministry, and by his death, burial, and resurrection.

Scripture teaches that Jesus is Lord—which means he is not just a human; he is also God with authority, control, and power over all.

Scripture teaches that Jesus is the Messiah—which means he is God's long promised King.

Jesus promised his followers that he would return one day to fully remove the effects of the curse and usher in the new age to come where sin, death, pain, and sadness are gone forever. This is the blessed hope for all disciples of Jesus. Until that time, Jesus offers humans a standing invitation into his "already-but-not-yet kingdom." He offers salvation to us by grace through faith. Grace is God's unearned favor where he offers us forgiveness and life in his kingdom, and we respond to his offer by faith, which is trusting and following Jesus.

Jesus spoke about the kingdom of God more than any other topic. His kingdom will be fully implemented over all creation when he returns—when everyone will say, he is "Lord of Lords and King of Kings" (Revelation 19:16).

1. When Jesus came, he announced the coming of his kingdom (Matthew 4:17). When a person turns to follow Jesus, they are added to God's kingdom. The apostle Paul describes what kingdom life in this world is like in the book of Romans:

> For the kingdom of God is not a matter of eating and drinking, but of righteousness, peace and joy in the Holy Spirit. (Romans 14:17)

Paul seems to be mimicking what he has heard from Jesus when he speaks about not being anxious or worrying about food or clothes. Jesus says in the book of Matthew:

> But seek first the kingdom of God and his righteousness, and all these things will be added to you. Therefore, do not be anxious about tomorrow, for tomorrow will be anxious for itself. Sufficient for the day is its own trouble. (Matthew 6:33–34, ESV)

What would your life look like if you were to more fully experience the righteousness, peace, and joy of the kingdom through the Holy Spirit as described in these passages?

_____

_____

_____

2. The kingdom has come, but it has not yet been fully revealed. When Jesus returns, it will be fully revealed to us. The following passage describes what will happen when Jesus returns:

> Brothers and sisters, we do not want you to be uninformed about those who sleep in death, so that you do not grieve like the rest of mankind, who have no hope. For we believe that Jesus died and rose again, and so we believe that God will bring with Jesus those who have fallen asleep in him. According to the Lord's word, we tell you that we who are still alive, who are left until the coming of the Lord, will certainly not precede those who have fallen asleep. For the Lord himself will come down from heaven, with a loud command, with the voice of the archangel and with the trumpet call of God, and the dead in Christ will rise first. After that, we who are still alive and are left will be caught up together with them in the clouds to meet the Lord in the air. And so we will be with the Lord forever. (1 Thessalonians 4:13–17)

What is Paul's desire for the Thessalonians? What needs to change in your life to help you have the same attitude as Paul?

_____

_____

_____

3. After Jesus returns, all human beings will stand before God for a final judgment of our lives. Those who trusted and followed Jesus will have their names in the Book of Life—a record of the saved.

> And I saw the dead, great and small, standing before the throne, and books were opened. Another book was opened, which is the book of life. The dead were judged according to what they had done as recorded in the books . . . Anyone whose name was not found written in the book of life was thrown into the lake of fire. (Revelation 20:12–15)

4. Then, after the final judgment, Jesus will take those who had faith in him to the new heaven and new earth, where the complete rule and reign of God over all nature will be complete. The book of Revelation describes the final reign of King Jesus this way:

> And I heard a loud voice from the throne saying, "Look! God's dwelling place is now among the people, and he will dwell with them. They will be his people, and God himself will be with them and be their God. He will wipe every tear from their eyes. There will be no more death or mourning or crying or pain, for the old order of things has passed away." (Revelation 21:3–4)

What do you think a kingdom like the one described will be like?

_____

_____

_____

5. **"Jesus is Lord." This was the earliest Christian confession. In the time of the Bible, a "lord" was someone with authority, control, or power over others.**

> Therefore God exalted him [Jesus] to the highest place and gave him the name that is above every name, that at the name of Jesus every knee should bow, in heaven and on earth and under the earth, and every tongue acknowledge that Jesus Christ is Lord, to the glory of God the Father. (Philippians 2:9–11)

What does it really mean to say, "Jesus is Lord"?

_____

_____

_____

6. **Disciple. It surprises many people to learn that the word "Christian" is only used three times in the Bible, but the word "disciple" is used about 270 times. In Matthew 4:19, Jesus says the following to two brothers, Peter and Andrew, while they are casting a net beside the Sea of Galilee:**

> Come, follow me, and I will make you fishers of men. (Matthew 4:19, ESV)

If we use this verse as a framework for understanding discipleship, we find three important attributes of a disciple. A disciple is a person who:

1. Is following Jesus *(head)*,
2. Is being changed by Jesus *(heart)*, and
3. Is committed to the mission of Jesus *(hands)*.

MINIMUM

This barrel is a good illustration of what it looks like to continue to live a faithful life of discipleship. Each stave (vertical plank) stands for a crucial area of being a disciple of Jesus. Faithfulness to Jesus involves these three core areas: following his leadership, being transformed by his Spirit, and prioritizing his disciple making mission in our lives. As we grow in one area, another area

becomes the new minimum. **Which part of this definition of a disciple is currently hardest to live out and why?**

_____

_____

_____

7. "Follow me." John 14:23–24 connects our obedience to Christ with our hearts and affections:

> Anyone who loves me will obey my teaching. My Father will love them, and we will come to them and make our home with them. Anyone who does not love me will not obey my teaching. (John 14:23–24)

Jesus lovingly rules our lives, and as he does, he replaces the falsehood we were handed from the world with his truth. In Mark 8:34–35, Jesus puts it starkly:

> Then he called the crowd to him along with his disciples and said: "Whoever wants to be my disciple must deny themselves and take up their cross and follow me. For whoever wants to save their life will lose it, but whoever loses their life for me and for the gospel will save it." (Mark 8:34–35)

What kind of help do you need to truly trust and follow Jesus as these passages describe?

_____

_____

_____

8. "And I will make you." 2 Corinthians 3:17–18 promises that God is transforming us from one degree of glory into another, into his image.

> Now the Lord is the Spirit, and where the Spirit of the Lord is, there is freedom. And we all, who with unveiled faces contemplate the Lord's glory, are being transformed into his image with ever-increasing glory, which comes from the Lord, who is the Spirit. (2 Corinthians 3:17–18)

What would it look like for your life to be truly transformed by the invisible Spirit?

_____

_____

_____

9. "Fishers of Men." Paul states it this way in 2 Corinthians 5:14–20:

> For Christ's love compels us, because we are convinced that one died for all, and therefore all died. And he died for all, that those who live should no longer live for themselves but for him who died for them and was raised again. So from now on we regard no one from a worldly point of view. Though we once regarded Christ in this way, we do so no longer. Therefore, if anyone is in Christ, the new creation has come: The old has gone, the new is here! All this is from God, who reconciled us to himself through Christ and gave us the ministry of reconciliation: that God was reconciling the world to himself in Christ, not counting people's sins against them. And he has committed to us the message of reconciliation. We are therefore Christ's ambassadors, as though God were making his appeal through us. We implore you on Christ's behalf: Be reconciled to God. (2 Corinthians 5:14–20)

We want to become more and more like Jesus. His mission was to give his life to save us, and he focused his ministry on making disciples. Jesus' disciples followed him and focused on sharing the message of salvation and making disciples.

Why is it important for us to share how Jesus reconciles people to God?

_____

_____

_____

10. "A Faithful Faith." Some people think "faith" is just believing that Jesus died for me. They think it is simply mental assent. But saving faith involves both trusting and following Jesus. A recent summary shows that 76 percent of Americans claim to be a Christian.[18] James describes true discipleship by describing what faith really means:

What good is it, my brothers and sisters, if someone claims to have faith but has no deeds? Can such faith save them? Suppose a brother or a sister is without clothes and daily food. If one of you says to them, "Go in peace; keep warm and well fed," but does nothing about their physical needs, what good is it? In the same way, faith by itself, if it is not accompanied by action, is dead. But someone will say, "You have faith; I have deeds." Show me your faith without deeds, and I will show you my faith by my deeds. You believe that there is one God. Good! Even the demons believe that—and shudder. (James 2:14–19)

Religion that is pure and undefiled before God the Father is this: to visit orphans and widows in their affliction, and to keep oneself unstained from the world. (James 1:27, ESV)

Paul, writing to the Galatian church, describes his interaction with the apostles in Jerusalem regarding the gospel being preached to both Jews and Gentiles. He reiterates the importance of faith that is lived out with action, faith that mimics the prophets of the Old Testament:

Only, they asked us to remember the poor, the very thing I was eager to do. (Galatians 2:10, ESV)

What does it look like for you to show that your life is based upon faith with deeds?

_____

_____

_____

Cultural Christianity	Biblical Discipleship
I like Jesus being a part of my life.	Jesus is the center of my life.
Following Jesus makes life easier.	Following Jesus requires obedience.
I believe that Jesus is *my* Savior.	Jesus is my Savior, Lord, and King.
I made a one-time decision.	I trust and follow Jesus daily.
I enjoy hearing and reading powerful messages that help me in life.	The Word of God transforms my actions.

Group Discussion Questions

1. How does the concept of the kingdom of God relate to Jesus' being both Messiah and Lord? Why is this significant for our faith?
2. Discuss the significance of obedience in following Jesus. What are a couple of ways that you want to obey God this week?
3. What are your thoughts about the final judgment and the hope found in Jesus?
4. Look back at the chart on Cultural Christianity and Biblical Discipleship. What are some ways you want to live out Biblical discipleship?

CHAPTER 7

Commitment

Key Theme: We make the commitment to turn to Jesus and place our faith in him through repentance, confession, and baptism.

The central teaching of the Bible is God reclaiming his relationship with us through Jesus (John 3:16; Romans 3:24–26). Jesus came into the world to rescue us, to be sacrificed as a sin offering, to bring us into his kingdom, and to guide and rule over us. God invites all of humanity to place their faith in him (John 3:16–18).

This is what it means when the Bible says that we are saved "by grace through faith" (Ephesians 2:8–9). Grace is a "free gift"—the unearned, eternal blessing of God. The fact that Christ died does not save people in and of itself, but it provides the ground upon which God, in full harmony with his holiness, is free to save those who have sinned against him.

The apostle Paul described God's great gift in Titus 3:3–7:

> At one time we too were foolish, disobedient, deceived and enslaved by all kinds of passions and pleasures. We lived in malice and envy, being hated and hating one another. But when the kindness and love of God our Savior appeared, he saved us, not because of righteous things we had done, but because of his mercy. He saved us through the washing of rebirth and renewal by the Holy Spirit, whom he poured out on us generously through Jesus Christ our Savior, so that, having been justified by his grace, we might become heirs having the hope of eternal life. (Titus 3:3–7)

This paragraph is a wonderful summary of the faith. It describes how God offers us his love, kindness, and mercy through Jesus. We are unable to save ourselves, but by God's mercy he saves us through a rebirth and renewal by the Holy Spirit. As a result, we respond by placing faith in Jesus.

1. The Bible teaches that we are made right with God when we place our faith in him. Review this summary:

We are made right in God's sight when we trust in Jesus Christ to take away our sins. And we all can be saved in this same way, no matter who we are or what we have done. For all have sinned; all fall short of God's glorious standard. Yet now God in his gracious kindness declares us not guilty. He has done this through Christ Jesus, who has freed us by taking away our sins. For God sent Jesus to take the punishment for our sins and to satisfy God's anger against us. We are made right with God when we believe that Jesus shed his blood, sacrificing his life for us. God was being entirely fair and just when he did not punish those who sinned in former times. And he is entirely fair and just in this present time when he declares sinners to be right in his sight because they believe in Jesus (Romans 3:22–26, NLT).

Many people have found that a simple acronym helps bring the biblical concept of faith into proper focus:

F	—	forsaking
A	—	all
I	—	I
T	—	take
H	—	him

What has putting your faith in Jesus looked like for you?

_____

_____

_____

2. Confession, Repentance, and Baptism. Let's go back to the setting of Acts 2, where the Christian faith is being publicly explained for the first time after Jesus' resurrection. Picture Peter as he tells them that Jesus Christ is the promised Messiah. He tells a Jewish crowd that it was the Jews themselves who cooperated with the Romans to put God's Messiah to death, but that God raised him from the dead. Peter tells them that Jesus Christ is now exalted at the right hand of God in heaven and that God is pouring out the Holy Spirit, as he promised long ago. Peter goes on to tell the people how they too can respond and place their faith in Jesus as Lord and Messiah.

"Therefore let all Israel be assured of this: God has made this Jesus, whom you crucified, both Lord and Messiah." When the people heard this, they were cut to the heart and said to Peter and the other apostles, "Brothers, what shall we do?"

Peter replied, "Repent and be baptized, every one of you, in the name of Jesus Christ for the forgiveness of your sins. And you will receive the gift of the Holy Spirit. The promise is for you and your children and for all who are far off—for all whom the Lord our God will call." With many other words he warned them; and he pleaded with them, "Save yourselves from this corrupt generation." Those who accepted his message were baptized, and about three thousand were added to their number that day. (Acts 2:36–41)

What did the first Christians do to express their commitment to faith in Jesus? Do you believe this applies today? Have you made such a decision?

_____

_____

_____

3. Faith is expressed in a confession. In its irreducible essence, faith is quite simple. It is the pledge in one's heart to trust and follow Jesus as your Lord. The following passage shows the fundamental core of the conversion experience. This confession was usually made in the water, just prior to baptism, as a verbal expression of the commitment to place one's faith in Jesus.[19]

That if you confess with your mouth, "Jesus is Lord," and believe in your heart that God raised him from the dead, you will be saved. For it is with your heart that you believe and are justified, and it is with your mouth that you confess and are saved. As the Scripture says, "Anyone who trusts in him will never be put to shame." (Romans 10:9–11)

When you declare that Jesus is Lord just before baptism, what are you saying?

_____

_____

_____

4. Faith is expressed in repentance. Repentance joins confession and baptism as an integral expression of saving faith. The Greek word in the New Testament for repentance, *metanoia*, literally means, "to have another mind" or, "a change of mind" that leads to a change in behavior.[20] The apostle Paul put it this way:

> In the past God overlooked such ignorance, but now he commands all people everywhere to repent. For he has set a day when he will judge the world with justice by the man he has appointed. He has given proof of this to all men by raising him from the dead. (Acts 17:30–31)

> First to those in Damascus, then to those in Jerusalem and in all Judea, and to the Gentiles also, I preached that they should repent and turn to God and prove their repentance by their deeds. (Acts 26:20)

Review the list of sins you marked in Chapter 3 on the sins of Galatians 5:19–21. What does it mean to personally show your repentance by your deeds as Acts 26:20 states?

_____

_____

_____

5. Water baptism in the Bible was intended to express faith in Jesus so we could receive the forgiveness of sins and the Holy Spirit. Water baptism was the God-given vehicle, or method, by which people appealed to Jesus Christ by faith for salvation. Water baptism plays the role of unifying faith, confession, repentance, and the call of discipleship—together in a concrete moment of personal commitment.[21]

Faith was the essential human response, and baptism was the concrete method of expressing faith in a holistic way. For those who want to learn more about baptism, I recommend the short book that Tony Twist, David Young, and I wrote, *Baptism: What the Bible Teaches.*[22] In the following passages, please note how faith is the essential human response and how baptism expresses faith as the ceremonial aspect of a concrete commitment.

> Then he said: "The God of our fathers has chosen you to know his will and to see the Righteous One and to hear words from his mouth . . . And now what are you waiting for? Get up, be baptized and wash your sins away, calling on his name." (Acts 22:14–16)

God waited patiently in the days of Noah while the ark was being built. In it only a few people, eight in all, were saved through water, and this water symbolizes baptism that now saves you also—not the removal of dirt from the body but the pledge of a good conscience toward God. It saves you by the resurrection of Jesus Christ, who has gone into heaven and is at God's right hand—with angels, authorities and powers in submission to him. (1 Peter 3:20–22)

What has it meant/will it mean to you to express faith in Jesus in baptism so your sins can be washed away as Scripture teaches?

_____

_____

_____

6. Water baptism in the Bible expressed the believer's personal commitment and was done by full immersion. The apostles described baptism as the point at which a person was saved because by doing that they were repenting and _pledging a good conscience to God_ (Acts 2:38; 1 Peter 3:21). The Greek word used in the New Testament for baptism is _baptizo_, which means "to dip, plunge, or to immerse." Romans 6:4–11 describes this pledge succinctly:

We were buried therefore with him by baptism into death in order that, just as Christ was raised from the dead by the glory of the Father, we too might walk in newness life. For if we have been united with him in a death like his, we shall certainly be united with him in a resurrection like his. We know that our old self was crucified with him in order that the body of sin might be brought to nothing, so that we would no longer be enslaved to sin. For one who has died has been set free from sin. Now if we have died with Christ, we believe that we will also live with him. We know that Christ, being raised from the dead, will never die again; death no longer has dominion over him. For the death he died he died to sin, once for all, but the life he lives he lives to God. So you must consider yourselves dead to sin but alive to God in Christ Jesus. (Romans 6:4–11, ESV)

Baptism, as re-enactment of the death, burial, and resurrection of Christ, must be by immersion of the believer.

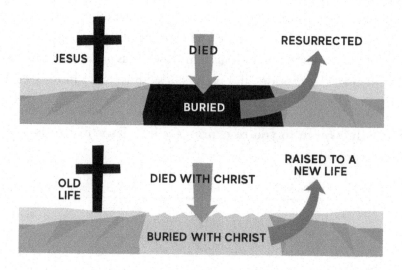

What does it mean for someone to die and be raised back to life with Christ in baptism?

_____

_____

_____

8. Making the commitment in our day. If we are seeking to follow the Bible, then we will teach that baptism is *the normative method* by which we make the commitment to turn from sin and place our faith in Christ. Baptism is given by God in the Bible as the prescribed way to do that for salvation.

Sometimes people use the "sinner's prayer" or tell people to "ask Jesus into your heart" to make this commitment. But as popular as these methods are, they are recent inventions, not found in any of the conversions recorded in the book of Acts—or in the rest of the Bible for that matter! They have really only been practiced by Christians during the last one hundred years.[23]

According to the Bible, the decision to become a Christian should be expressed in water baptism as the concrete means given by God. In this sense, we must reclaim the teaching that baptism—as an expression of faith in Jesus—is "for the remission of sins," as both the Bible (Acts 2:38) and the earliest Christian statements of faith, like the Nicene Creed, teach.[24]

God looks at the heart and often saves people who do not know about this *normative way*. But why live in the realm of exceptions to the norm? Why not just follow the Bible? It's way better to rely on the teachings of the Word of God than on human inventions.

People responded to the gospel and were baptized immediately in the Bible. They were baptized right away on the day of Pentecost, after hearing about Christ's salvation for the first time in a big crowd (Acts 2:38–42). An Ethiopian man did it immediately after understanding the teaching of Scripture, even in the midst of a long trip through the wilderness (Acts 8:36–40). A jailer even temporarily took his prisoners out of the jail in the middle of the night (Paul and Silas) so that he and his family could be immediately baptized (Acts 16:31–33). We should have that same sense of urgency today.

Water baptism seals and holistically solidifies our commitment to trust and follow Jesus—and thus become a Christian. It is the believer's spiritual wedding ceremony commitment to Christ. In the Bible, this was the special time in which the miracle of salvation typically occurred. We seek to restore and follow this normative practice in our day.

9. If you haven't been baptized, what is holding you back? If you have been baptized, how can you help others to follow this teaching?

Group Discussion Questions

1. What does it look like to live a life that recognizes the grace of God?
2. Explore the acronym "FAITH" ("Forsaking all, I take him"). How does this summarize the biblical view of faith? Discuss its significance in relation to salvation.
3. Consider the passage from Acts 2:36–41. What are the normative practices of the first-century church that apply to salvation today?
4. What is the connection between baptism and the gospel story? Look back at the first chapter and review the seven essential elements and how they connect to baptism.

CHAPTER 8

Discipleship

Key Theme: We live as disciples (followers of Jesus) by relying on God's Spirit and participating in a local church.

We were created for a relationship with God, and commitment to be disciples of Jesus is the form or shape by which we pursue that goal. Stated differently, we were created to have a relationship with God the Father, *where we live by faith as disciples of his Son, Jesus Christ, in the power of his Spirit.*

A disciple is simply "a follower," "a student," or better, "an apprentice."[25] A Christian is "an apprentice" of Jesus Christ who is *learning from him* how to develop a deep and meaningful relationship with God. This was the original mandate that Jesus gave to his apostles.

> Therefore go and make disciples of all nations, baptizing them in the name of the Father and of the Son and of the Holy Spirit, and teaching them to obey everything I have commanded you. And surely I am with you always, to the very end of the age. (Matthew 28:19–20)

The goal of Jesus' first disciples was to "make disciples" of all nations. Jesus' call was at the same time an invitation to salvation and a summons to imitation and service.[26]

A person simply cannot be a Christian without being a disciple.[27] It would be like trying to be a human without breathing. A Christian is spiritually dead if they are not (on some level) a follower of Jesus. This truth is described in various ways (not always by using the term "disciple"). It is a major, fundamental, and underlying theme of the entire New Testament.[28] God has saved us through faith in Jesus Christ (Romans 3:22–25), and now God is transforming us into the image of Jesus Christ (2 Corinthians 3:16–17). God has predetermined that all things in our lives will work toward this end.

The apostle Paul stated it succinctly: "For those God foreknew he also predestined to be conformed to the likeness of his Son" (Romans 8:29).

The writer C. S. Lewis says:

> It is easy to think that the Church has a lot of different objects—education, building, missions, holding services . . . Church exists for nothing else but to draw men into Christ, to make them little Christs. If they are not doing that, all the cathedrals, clergy, missions, sermons, even the Bible itself, are simply a waste of time. God became Man for no other purpose.[29]

Dietrich Bonhoeffer was just as clear in his description:

> Discipleship means adherence to Christ and, because Christ is the object of that adherence, it must take the form of discipleship.[30]

If we are to truly live as faithful disciples, we need to give and receive training, help, encouragement, and support so that we can learn how to become more and more like Jesus Christ. That is how the disciples of Jesus changed, and in turn, changed the world.

What a high calling it is to be a disciple of Jesus! You might say, "I know my weaknesses, and I am sure to stumble and fall. I want to live this way, but I do not have the ability."

"Yes," God answers, "you do not have the ability, but I will help you as I give to you my people, my power, and my Spirit."

So we can say with confidence, "God is my helper, and he will enable me to truly follow Jesus. I will not do it perfectly, and I will often stumble and fall, but by God's grace working in me, I will make it."

1. In Acts 2, after the people had repented of their sins and been baptized, they gathered together as a church. Look at the following description of that church:

> They devoted themselves to the apostles' teaching and to fellowship, to the breaking of bread and to prayer. Everyone was filled with awe at the many wonders and signs performed by the apostles. All the believers were together and had everything in common. They sold property and possessions to give to anyone who had need. Every day they continued to meet together in the temple courts. They broke bread in their homes and ate together with glad and sincere hearts, praising God and enjoying the favor of all the people. And the Lord added to their number daily those who were being saved. (Acts 2:42–47)

How would you describe the early church and the people in it? How does this differ from your church experience?

_____

_____

_____

2. If we are willing, God helps us to live as disciples of Jesus through his Holy Spirit, who lives within the Christian.

> For this reason I kneel before the Father, from whom every family in heaven and on earth derives its name. I pray that out of his glorious riches he may strengthen you with power through his Spirit in your inner being, so that Christ may dwell in your hearts through faith. (Ephesians 3:14–17)

How have you seen God strengthen you with power through his Spirit?

_____

_____

_____

3. Prayer is vital for us because that is how we commune with God. Most of us need help to effectively pray. The Lord's Prayer—used as a prayer outline—is a very effective prayer model. I have used it with great benefit daily for over twenty-five years.

It is taken from Matthew 6:9–13 as a model for us to use when praying. As you read, be sure to pause and practice this prayer.

Our Father in heaven, hallowed be your name,

> God, you are holy, separate from us, and morally pure. Let us take a few moments to pray about making you and your name pure in our minds and lives.

Your kingdom come, your will be done, on earth as it is in heaven.

God, we look forward to Jesus' return when your kingdom will be fully established. Let us take a few moments and place our hope in the merging of heaven and earth in the new heavens and new earth that you are bringing to us.

Give us today our daily bread.

We trust you for today. You teach us that today has enough in it to just focus on that. Provide for our basic needs today. Let us take a few moments to express them to you now.

Forgive us our debts,

God, we are sinful people, even though we try not to sin. As we reflect for a few moments, please forgive the following sins . . .

As we also have forgiven our debtors.

God, you teach us that we must forgive as we have been forgiven. We now reflect on those we need to forgive, and we forgive them.

And lead us not into temptation but deliver us from the evil one.

As we take a few moments to think about upcoming struggles, help us, Lord! Guide us away from things that will tempt us. Protect us from Satan in the upcoming challenges.

Prayer draws us closer to God. What hinders you in your prayers, and in what way could this model help you?

_____

_____

_____

4. God gives us church leaders to help us "grow up" and "mature." The apostle Paul described his ministry as a leader in God's church in this light:

> We proclaim him, admonishing and teaching everyone with all wisdom, so that we may present everyone perfect in Christ. To this end I labor, struggling with all his energy, which so powerfully works in me. (Colossians 1:28–29)

> You show that you are a letter from Christ, the result of our ministry, written not with ink but with the Spirit of the living God, not on tablets of stone but on tablets of human hearts. (2 Corinthians 3:3)

> My dear children, for whom I am again in the pains of childbirth until Christ is formed in you, how I wish I could be with you now and change my tone, because I am perplexed about you! (Galatians 4:19–20)

How can church leaders help you to more fully mature in trusting and following Jesus?

_____

_____

_____

5. Church is essential for faithful disciples, as the Bible tells us, because Christians need to spur one another on to be and to do what Jesus wants us to be and to do.

> See to it, brothers and sisters, that none of you has a sinful, unbelieving heart that turns away from the living God. But encourage one another daily, as long as it is called "Today," so that none of you may be hardened by sin's deceitfulness. We have come to share in Christ, if indeed we hold our original conviction firmly to the very end. (Hebrews 3:12–14)

> And let us consider how we may spur one another on toward love and good deeds. Let us not give up meeting together, as some are in the habit of doing, but let us encourage one another—and all the more as you see the Day approaching. (Hebrews 10:23–25)

Do you have negative experiences that make it difficult to be committed to your local church? If so, how can you heal enough to get involved?

_____

_____

_____

_____

6. Jesus' method of discipleship was grounded in the environment of "agape love," also described as "Jesus-like love." This kind of love is a love that acts according to what is best for the other person. Jesus loved people this way and he commands us to show this same kind of love for one another. He describes it for us in John 13:34–35:

> A new command I give you: Love one another. As I have loved you, so you must love one another. By this everyone will know that you are my disciples, if you love one another. (John 13:34–35)

Is it easy for you to give and receive this kind of love? Why is it so important in the local church?

_____

_____

_____

7. As Christians, God has given us all responsibilities to serve others. We do this in different ways, but especially in the local church. A simple passage teaching this concept is Romans 12. Notice what Paul says here. He tells us that each of us—regular, everyday Christians—is part of the body of Christ (the church), and we are members of each other. We belong to one another.

> For just as each of us has one body with many members, and these members do not all have the same function, so in Christ we, though many, form one body, and each member belongs to all the others. We have different gifts, according to the grace given to each of us. If your gift is prophesying, then prophesy in accordance with your faith; if it is serving, then serve; if it is teaching, then teach; if it is to encourage, then give encouragement; if it is giving,

then give generously; if it is to lead, do it diligently; if it is to show mercy, do it cheerfully. (Romans 12:4–8)

Why is it important to use one's gifts to serve others, especially in the church?

_____

_____

_____

8. In addition to giving our time and efforts, the Bible teaches us that we should be generous. The Bible often points to a standard of 10 percent as a good goal but not a law. The more important focus is to give generously, from the heart, not reluctantly, as one giving back to God.

> Remember this: Whoever sows sparingly will also reap sparingly, and whoever sows generously will also reap generously. Each of you should give what you have decided in your heart to give, not reluctantly or under compulsion, for God loves a cheerful giver. And God is able to bless you abundantly, so that in all things at all times, having all that you need, you will abound in every good work. (2 Corinthians 9:6–8)

Giving cheerfully is important to God. Why do you think this is, and why is it especially important in our finances?

_____

_____

_____

As we end this study, what is the next step for you on your journey with God, and are you willing to commit to doing it with us now?

_____

_____

_____

_____

_____

_____

_____

_____

_____

_____

_____

_____

Group Discussion Questions

1. Re-examine Acts 2:42–47. What are characteristics of God's church? If you were to start a church congregation, which aspects would you begin with?
2. What are some ways that you can train someone this week in one area of disciple making? Explore the idea of training a group with the model found at the beginning of this workbook.
3. Take a few minutes as a group to pray about multiplication of disciples and God's kingdom vision. What sort of dreams do you have for disciple making in your group?
4. Examine the Bible study methods in Appendix I and discuss as a group how the Bible is your curriculum for disciple making. Which book of the Bible would be best for your group to study?

Transformation Group Resources

THE DISCIPLESHIP GROUP COVENANT (AGREEMENT)

In order to grow toward maturity in Christ and be changed by the truth of God's Word in transparent community, I commit to the following:

1. **ENGAGE:** I will engage in this group and seek to grow in my understanding of Jesus and what it means to trust and follow him (even if I am not a Christian and do not plan to become one).
2. **COMMIT:** I commit to attending every gathering. I will be there on time and come with my work completed. I will finish the course and stay with the group. I understand that we are investing in each other, and I commit myself to this group.
3. **JESUS-STYLE:** This group will be about Kingdom Teachings and Kingdom Doings. We will imitate Jesus in intentional and relational disciple making. To help us enter fully into this group process, we will seek to follow Jesus' rhythms each month (Learn, Eat, Serve, Rest).
4. **LIFE-CHANGING ACCOUNTABILITY:** I recognize I need life-changing accountability, so I will seek to be open about myself and my relationship with God for learning and growing in my walk with him. To foster an environment based upon Scripture and Jesus Christ in the context of community, I commit to total confidentiality; I won't share what is said confidentially with anyone, even my spouse.
5. **MULTIPLICATION:** I commit that after _____ months, I will support the multiplication of this group, and I will prayerfully consider leading a group like this myself.

_____ _____
Signature   Signature

_____ _____
Signature   Signature

SHARING OUR SPIRITUAL AUTOBIOGRAPHIES[31]

This is a guide for sharing our spiritual autobiographies. The one who began praying for this group should start and set the example.

Divide into decades – Draw a horizontal line on a piece of paper and divide that line into sections with shorter vertical lines, creating one section for each decade of your life. We'll call it your "lifeline."

Now, ask God to remind you of critical events, turning points, moments of truth, disasters, failures, victories . . . the *really important, life-shaping events that happened in each of these decades.* Put a number on the scale to mark your age when it happened. Put it *above the horizontal line* if it was a *positive* event, and put it *below the line* if it was a *negative* one. It might look like this:

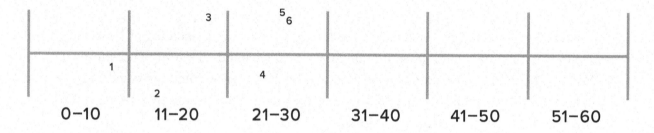

| 0–10 | 11–20 | 21–30 | 31–40 | 41–50 | 51–60 |

Notes on our example lifeline:

1. My dad abandoned our family (nine years old).
2. My mom was diagnosed with breast cancer (thirteen years old).
3. I was baptized (nineteen years old).

The God part . . .

Beside each of your notes, jot down where God, as you understand him, was in each of these moments. Be completely honest. Here's how notes might look on the example above . . .

Event	**God**
1. My dad abandoned our family.	1. I didn't know God then. I felt alone, abandoned, and unloved.
2. My mom was diagnosed with breast cancer.	2. I thought, "If there is a God, how could he be good?" I turned away in anger and unbelief.
3. I was baptized.	3. God worked in me to really grow me in service to him and love for his church.

Our goal as we tell our stories is to share our thoughts and let people know us. After you've added the God part to each major event, you'll end with a statement of where you are *right now*. For example: "I have committed to this group to grow closer to Jesus, but I don't feel worthy. I'm not sure where this will lead me, but I'm in this with you guys."

EXTRA RESOURCES

Definitions

Here are some key definitions we believe are vitally important. If we are going to have a culture of disciple making, we must agree on what it means to be a disciple and make disciples.

1. **Disciple** – someone who is (1) following Jesus, (2) being changed by Jesus, and (3) is committed to the mission of Jesus (Matthew 4:19, ESV).

   And he said to them, "[1] Follow me, and [2] I will make you [3] fishers of men."

2. **Disciple making** – entering into relationships to intentionally help people follow Jesus, be changed by Jesus, and join the mission of Jesus (Matthew 4:19). Another definition from the Great Commission is that disciple making is about helping people (1) trust and (2) follow Jesus (Matthew 28:19–20a, ESV).

   Go therefore and make disciples of all nations, [1] baptizing them in the name of the Father and of the Son and of the Holy Spirit, [2] teaching them to observe all that I have commanded you.

3. **Disciple maker** – a disciple of Jesus who enters into relationships with people to intentionally help them follow Jesus, be changed by Jesus, and join the mission of Jesus, *or* a disciple of Jesus who enters into relationships with people to help them trust and follow Jesus.

DISCOVERY BIBLE STUDY OUTLINE

A — Ask	B — Bible	C — Commit

What is one thing that happened last week for which you are thankful?
 	
What is one struggle or worry you are dealing with in your life, family, or community?
 	
[Prayer]
 	
How did you do with applying and sharing last week's lesson?
	Read this week's text out loud.
	
	Retell the passage in your own words.
	
	Discuss:
	
	1. What do we learn about God from this passage?
	   – How have you seen this in your life?
	
	2. What do we learn about people from this passage?
	   – How have you seen this in your life?
	
	*Think: How would my life change if I put this passage into practice?
		1. How will I put this passage into practice this week?
		* **I will . . .**
		
		2. Who needs to hear this passage this week?
		* **I will share this passage with . . .**

THREE-THIRDS BIBLE STUDY OUTLINE

Look Back	Look Up	Look Forward
This is relational accountability. Be vulnerable and honest: • What are you grateful/thankful for? • How have you obeyed God in the last week? • Whom did you pray with or share God's story with? • Find a way to worship together as a group (pray, sing, journal, etc.).	This is learning to be transformed by the Word of God. Let the text transform your actions: Read this week's text out loud. Retell the passage in your own words. Discuss: 1. What do we learn about God and people from this passage? 2. How would my life change if I put this passage into practice?	This is intentional planning for spiritual growth: Practice retelling the story as preparation for sharing it with others. Whom will you share the story with this week? When? How? (Set goals and pray.) Vision: What is God doing through you and through this group for his kingdom purposes? Is there anything we need to prepare for?

EXTRA RESOURCES

Commitments

Transformation is achieved by imitating the practices of Jesus. These practices are also known as spiritual disciplines. In our groups, we want to end each week with each person committing to practicing one small discipline they need to do to help them grow in their discipleship. The next week, we can begin our time checking on how we did in our commitment.

Each member of the group ought to come up with their own commitment, although sometimes a group may all decide to practice the same discipline. Feel free to be creative based on what you need. Many times it may be helpful if the commitment aligns in some way with the discussion that day.

When we make commitments, we must make them like **SAM**. Every commitment should be:

Specific – We are more likely to keep to the commitment if it's specific. "I want to pray for five minutes every morning before I eat breakfast" is better than "I want to pray more."

Attainable – Think small and realistically; this is a long journey. "I want to have one spiritual conversation with a classmate this week" is better than "I want to baptize three people this week."

Measurable – If other group members can't measure it, it's tough to have accountability. "I want to write down a way I saw God that day in my journal each night this week" is better than "I want to see God more."

Examples:

- This week I will send an encouraging text to three people.
- Each night, I'll make a schedule for the next day and plan for time with God.
- I will do ten push-ups every time I use profanity in my speech.
- I will read one chapter of my Bible every weekday at 7:30 a.m.

Some Ideas for Kingdom Doings

Jesus not only taught about the kingdom, but he also lived out what God's kingdom is like (see Matthew 4:23 and 9:35). For example, Matthew 5–7 describes Kingdom Teaching; Matthew 8–9 describes Kingdom Doing. We want to imitate Jesus in his Kingdom Teachings and Kingdom Doings. Every third week, we will do a Kingdom Doing as a group. These are built upon the rhythms of Jesus's disciple making, but we can be creative in these as well. You may come up with ideas as a group.

Examples:

- Going to a park with natural scenery, spreading out, and spending time with God in silence and solitude, then coming back together after an hour to talk about it
- Visiting a hospital and looking for people to pray with, perhaps in a waiting room or cafeteria
- Having a game night with your group, and each of you inviting someone who could use community or who may not know the Lord
- Going to a prayer labyrinth
- Driving down the road together, looking for someone who may need help in some way
- Enjoying a meal together, perhaps inviting someone whom others may not invite often

Three Classic Arguments for God's Existence

O ur world presents a view of life that often assumes there is no God. The presentation of scientific perspectives, for example, often assumes there is no God. This is ironic because the majority of scientists still believe in God.

The biggest barrier to belief in God is the view that evolution explains everything and that the teaching of the Bible is in conflict with the hard facts upon which evolution is based. But once people see that the hard facts of earth history can be harmonized with the teaching of the Bible, most objections melt away. The interpretation of the creation account in Genesis and the integration of the facts of earth history is an area where Christian scholars disagree with each other. It is not an essential element of the faith, nor an important element upon which a church needs to take a stand (as long as one holds to a high view of scripture), but it is a personal element of the faith, where different Christians will take different positions, even within a local congregation.

But Christian scholars tend to agree that the evidence that God made the universe is very strong. The evidence becomes a basis by which we can make strong arguments for God's existence.

There are three classic arguments that demonstrate God's existence on these objective grounds.[32] The names for the arguments are *cosmological, teleological, and moral,* and I will simplify them into three questions:

1. How was the universe created?
2. Where did the complexity of life come from?
3. What makes something morally right or wrong?

I. How Was the Universe Created?

I (Bobby) personally find Big Bang cosmology to be convincing. I know that it is not for everyone (it is in that third area of elements where Christians differ from each other). Regardless of when it happened, I'm convinced that God created this world.

I grew up near the Rocky Mountains of Western Canada. As a teenager, I would often spend weekends in the winter skiing. Sometimes, I would look out over the mountains from a chair on the ski lift. The tall, snow-capped mountains were ruggedly set against the backdrop of the light-blue sky and filled with beautiful evergreen trees. The scenes were simply majestic. In such breathtaking moments, I would think to myself, *Wow, God made this!* I could not imagine that such a world "just happened" by chance.

Most of us share these sentiments. We look at the world and ask, "Where else could this have come from?" Something made this world. Our natural reaction is to say, "God made it."

Prior to emergence of the Big Bang theory, many scientists believed the universe was infinitely old. And I personally accept that science has now demonstrated that the universe had a beginning. Astronomers and astrophysicists are now convinced that the universe—and all time, space, matter, and energy—literally sprang into existence *out of nothing*.[33] The universe began with a "Big Bang." As one scientist stated, "Almost everyone now believes that the universe, and time itself, had a beginning at the Big Bang."[34]

Before the "Big Bang," the universe and everything else did not exist. There was no time, no matter, no energy, and no space. Stop and think about these facts for a moment. The implications are astounding:

- There was no yesterday, no today, no tomorrow, no beginning, and no end.
- There were no dimensions: no up, no down, no back, no front.
- There was no matter, no atoms, no elements of any kind.
- There was no physical energy, power, or motion.

Absolutely nothing physical existed. Nothing! Then, literally out of nowhere, everything that physically exists sprang into existence. There was a "Big Bang" and everything that exists was created in that instant. As William Lane Craig says, "Physical space and time were created in that event, as well as all the matter and energy in the universe."[35]

In every other realm, we know that "something" cannot come from "nothing." So where did the universe come from?

Think for a moment about the possible options! If all physical elements were created in the moment of the Big Bang, they could only have been created by something non-physical. There is only one good answer: God. Only a non-material being like God could create the physical universe. Only God is invisible, eternal, and all-powerful. As the Bible says, "by faith we understand that the universe was formed at God's command, so that what is seen was not made out of what was visible" (Hebrews 11:3).

Philosophers have developed a very simple summary of the "Big Bang" argument for God's existence:[36]

- Whatever begins to exist had a cause.
- The universe began to exist.
- *Therefore*, the universe had a cause (God).

The person who does not believe in God is in trouble at this point. How can they explain the beginning of the universe? It seems to me that if someone were an advocate for the Big Bang theory and did not believe in God, they must believe that the universe came from nothing and by nothing.

At this point, thoughtful people often ask, "Well then who made God?" It is a good question, except it misses one key point: if something begins to exist, it must have a source. But God never had a beginning, so he never needed to have a source. Something does not come from nothing. A being must have always existed from which material things came into existence. Yet the Big Bang teaches us that this something could not have been limited by matter or time. The cause of the universe must be non-material and unlimited by time (what the Bible calls "eternal").

The Bible teaches that the creation of the universe is the work of God. In fact, the first verses of the Bible could not be clearer: "In the beginning God created the heavens and the earth" (Genesis 1:1).

II. Where Did the Complexity of Life Come From?

The creation of the universe set the stage for the creation of life on planet earth. Scientists tell us that the simplest forms of life appeared on planet earth soon after it formed.[37] But as we will see below, without God it is hard to find a good explanation for the creation of complex biological life.

Biologists and biochemists have tried to explain the origin of life in different naturalistic ways (without God), but the more we learn about biological life, the more we find that a miracle was required for it to have started. Stated differently, if we assume that there is no God, we are at a loss to explain the creation of life.

Scientists used to think they could replicate the creation of life in a laboratory. They have now given up on such projects—they do not have a clue about how to create life from non-living materials.

Harold Morowitz was a mathematical biologist who specialized in this field. He said that if you take all the possibilities or random combinations from the beginning of time until now, it is impossible to find a mathematical model that will explain the creation of life.[38] He said that the random assembly of the most basic building blocks of life, including something as simple as a functional protein called "biological self-replicating systems," is unexplainable.

Scientists try in various ways to describe the odds of the simplest blocks of life forming by chance (without God). Consider the following analogies that have been put forward to explain the creation of biological life:

- The odds of the building blocks of life "just happening by chance" are the same as a Boeing 747 being created accidentally by a tornado whirling through a junkyard.[39]
- The odds of the building blocks of life "just happening by chance" are the same as a man finding the same grain of sand after being blindfolded and randomly dropped in the Sahara Desert—three different times.[40]
- The odds of the building blocks of life "just happening by chance" are the same as believing that monkeys typing on computers could randomly create the entire thirty-volume *Encyclopedia Britannica* without error.[41]

Leading scientists have used each of the statements above to explain the impossible odds required for the spontaneous creation of the building blocks of life. The appearance of life on the planet is a miracle that points to God.[42]

The argument for God's existence, as presented so far, can be summed up in a few simple points:

- Biological life resulted either by chance or by design.
- The odds that life began by chance are so small as to be equal to zero.
- Therefore, life began by design (by God).

Stated differently, the belief that God created life is the most satisfying explanation for the complexity of simple biological life.[43]

III. What Makes Something Morally Right or Wrong?

The last classic argument asks you to look deeply into your own heart. Do you believe that there are some things that are truly right or wrong? This is called the moral argument for God, and its most popular form was given by C. S. Lewis in *Mere Christianity*.[44]

Here is my summary of his argument:

1. There must be an objective source for the moral laws we sense or else:

   - We would not feel certain that some things are *morally wrong* (moral disagreements would have no real logical ground).
   - Our moral critiques, where we say, "That is wrong," would be meaningless.
   - There would be no real necessity to keep promises or treaties.
   - We would not feel the need to make excuses for breaking moral laws (e.g., saying, "I am sorry that I lied").

2. But a universal moral law requires a universal Moral Law Giver (God):

   - If God is behind our sense that *some things are just right or wrong*, then it becomes objective.
   - Then, God made us to intuitively know that *some things are just right or wrong* (e.g., that killing is wrong).
   - That means that God cares about our behavior, and we intuitively sense this to be true.

3. Further, God, as the universal Moral Law Giver, must be good:

   - Our strong sense that *some things are right and wrong* is our intuitive appeal that "Good" is "out there."
   - Our appeal to the Good is ultimately an appeal to an objective standard of the Good, which can only be God.

4. Therefore, there must be an absolutely good Moral Law Giver who is God.

In the book *Reasonable Faith*, William Lane Craig shows how we cannot truly live with the reality of atheism.[45] If there is no God, then the following things are true:

   - There is no ultimate meaning to life.
   - There is no ultimate right or wrong in life.
   - There is no ultimate purpose to life.

This is a very depressing viewpoint. I have never met anyone who can truly live a life of hope and joy and believe these things.

In the end, you will have to ask yourself about these arguments. I personally find them to be compelling. I have laid them out as formal arguments so that you can grapple with them at a logical level.

But personally, I have found them to be true at a basic intuitive level. I have always found myself thinking in a simpler way:

- The world must have been created by God.
- The complexity of life can only be explained by God.
- My sense of right and wrong must be based on God.

It is because I first believed these things that I was open to what Jesus taught in the Bible. And then, when I came to see for myself what Jesus taught, he captured the best of my heart, mind, soul, and strength. I hope you will be open to letting Jesus do the same for you. *That* is the true purpose of life.

1. See Garth M. Rosell, *Boston's Historic Park Street Church: The Story of an Evangelical Landmark* (Grand Rapids, MI: Kregel Publications, 2009), 13.

2. This material is drawn in large part from Jason Dukes, *Inviting Along: Five Shifts to Help You Move from Informational to Relational Disciple Making* (Discipleship.org, 2018). This handout is an edited version by Dr. Carl Williamson and Grant Fitzhugh.

3. Albert Mohler, president of Southern Theological Seminary, arrived at a similar proposal to the one I advocate here, which I adopted in the late 1990s. See Albert Mohler, "A Call for Theological Triage and Christian Maturity," May 20, 2004, albertmohler.com/2004/05/20/a-call-for-theological-triage-and-christian-maturity-2, accessed December 2014.

4. See Matthew Bates, *Gospel Allegiance* (Brazos, 2019).

5. Lawrence Mykytiuk, "Did Jesus Exist? Searching for Evidence Beyond the Bible," *Biblical Archaeology Review* (January/February 2015): 45–51, 76.

6. N. T. Wright, *Simply Good News: Why the Gospel is News and What Makes It Good* (HarperOne, 2015), 58–59.

7. William Lane Craig may be the foremost expert on the evidence for the resurrection of Jesus. See his summary article at reasonablefaith.org/the-resurrection-of-jesus, accessed November 28, 2016.

8. Josephus *Ag. Ap.* 2.204; see Craig Evans, *Jesus and the Remains of His Day* (Hendrickson Publishing, 2015), 70.

9. See Evans, *Jesus and the Remains of His Day* and Ann Spangler and Lois Tverberg, *Sitting at the Feet of Rabbi Jesus: How the Jewishness of Jesus Can Transform Your Faith* (Grand Rapids, MI: Zondervan, 2009), 24.

10. For more on the connection between oral tradition and the Gospels, see Craig Blomberg, *The Historical Reliability of the Gospels*, 2nd ed. (Downers Grove: IVP Academic, 2014), 57–61.

11. Craig Blomberg, *Can We Still Believe the Bible? An Evangelical Engagement with Contemporary Questions.* (Brazos Press, 2014). See also Michael Kruger, *The Question of Canon* (Downers Grove, IL: InterVarsity Press, 2013). Michael Kruger, *Canon Revisited: Establishing the Origins and Authority of the New Testament Books* (Wheaton, IL: Crossway, 2012).

12. R. C. Sproul, *The Holiness of God* (Wheaton, IL: Tyndale House Publishers, 1985), 53.

13. We cannot understand God or the Bible until we understand that God is holy! This is probably why when Jesus taught us a model prayer—the Lord's Prayer—that prayer began with the petition for God's name to be held "holy." We pray, "Our Father in heaven, *hallowed* be your name" (Matthew 6:9). This prayer draws us to the heart of God: his name must be held up among us as "holy."

14. A. T. Robertson, *Word Pictures*, vol. 14, 525.

15. This line of thought is drawn from one of my former Bible College teachers, Jimmy Allen, *Survey of Romans* (Searcy, AR: Harding College Press, 1973; rev. ed., 1976), 31.

16. C. E. B. Cranfield, *Romans: A Shorter Commentary* (Grand Rapids, MI: Eerdmans, 1985), 211–212.

17. Scot McKnight, *Kingdom Conspiracy* (Grand Rapids, MI: Brazos, 2014) for an in-depth presentation of what follows.

18. As late as 2010, up to 85 percent of Americans claimed to be Christian, though it had fallen to 76 percent by 2015. See George Barna, *Futurecast: What Today's Trends Mean for Tomorrow's World* (Carol Stream, IL: Tyndale, 2011), Kindle location 124. See also the Navigators, *The State of Discipleship* (Tyndale, 2015).

19. See Cranfied, *Romans*, 257. In regard to Romans 10:9–10, he states, "It seems clear that 'Jesus is Lord' was already an established confession formula. It is probable that it was used in connection with baptism . . ."

20. For more information see Walter Bauer, *A Greek-English Lexicon of the New Testament and Other Early Christian Literature*, 2nd. ed., revised by William Arndt and F. Wilbur Gingrich (Chicago: University of Chicago Press, 1979).

21. The position on the meaning of baptism, which is sketched out here, is the earliest Christian understanding of baptism, reflected in the writing of Christians in the first centuries. See the Nicene Creed of AD 381 in *The Creeds of Christendom*, 3 Volumes, edited by Philip Schaff (Grand Rapids, MI: Baker Book House, 1996). For a technical and scholarly support, Everett Ferguson: *Baptism in the Early Church: History, Theology, and Liturgy in the First Five Centuries* (Grand Rapids, MI: Wm. B. Eerdmans Publishing Co., 2009). For information on the historical heritage of this view see David Fletcher (editor), *Baptism and the Remission of Sins: An Historical Perspective* (Joplin, MO: College Press, 1990).

22. Tony Twist, Bobby Harrington, and David Young, *Baptism: What the Bible Teaches* (Renew, 2019) available on Renew.org or through Amazon.com.

23. See Paul Chitwood, *The Sinner's Prayer: An Historic and Theological Analysis* (PhD Dissertation, Southern Baptist Theological Seminary, 2001).

24. The Nicene Creed of AD 381 states "I acknowledge one Baptism for the remission of sins." See *The Creeds of Christendom*, 3 Volumes, edited by Philip Schaff (Grand Rapids, MI: Baker Book House, 1996).

25. Dallas Willard, "How To Be A Disciple," *Christian Century* (April 22–29, 1998): 430–431. See also, Dallas Willard, *The Divine Conspiracy* (San Francisco: Harper and Row, 1997).

26. Michael Wilkins, *Following the Master: A Biblical Theology of Discipleship* (Grand Rapids, MI: Zondervan Publishing, 1992), 186.

27. See this point explained in the definitive Biblical study on discipleship in Wilkins, *Following the Master*.

28. See Richard Longenecker (editor), *Patterns of Discipleship in the New Testament* (Grand Rapids, MI: Eerdmans, 1996).

29. C. S. Lewis, *Mere Christianity* (New York: Simon & Schuster, 1996), 171.

30. Dietrich Bonhoeffer, *The Cost of Discipleship* (New York: Touchstone, 1995), 59.

31. This material was developed by Radical Mentoring and is edited and used by Bobby Harrington and Carl Williamson with Regi Campbell's explicit permission.

32. See the helpful summary of most of the arguments for God's existence in Norman Geisler, *The Big Book of Christian Apologetics* (Ada, MI: Baker Books, 2012).

33. Michael D. Lemonick, "Cosmic Fingerprint," *Time* (Feb. 24, 2003): 45.

34. Stephen Hawking and Roger Penrose, *The Nature of Time and Space* (Princeton Univ. Press, 1996), 20.

35. William Lane Craig, "Why I Believe God Exists," in *Why I Am a Christian, eds. Norman L. Geisler and Paul K. Hoffman* (Baker, 2001), 63.

36. Ibid. and J. P. Moreland, *Scaling the Secular City* (Grand Rapids, MI: Baker Books, 1987).

37. John M. Hayes, "The Earliest Memories of Life on Earth," *Nature* 384 (1996): 21–22. See also S. J. Mojzsis et al., "Evidence for Life on Earth before 3,800 Million Years Ago," *Nature* 384 (1996): 55–59; J. William Schopf, "Microfossils of the Early Archean Apex Chert: New Evidence of the Antiquity of Life," *Science* 260 (1993): 640–46.

38. H. Morowitz, "Biological Self-Replicating Systems," in *Progress in Theoretical Biology*, ed. F. Snell (New York: Academic Press, 1967), 35ff.

39. Fred Hoyle, *The Intelligent Universe* (Joseph, 1983).

40. This statement is quoted in Lee Strobel, *The Case for Faith* (Grand Rapids, MI: Zondervan, 2000).

41. Quoted in Lee Strobel, *The Case for Faith*, 110.

42. Francis Crick, *Life Itself: Its Origin and Nature* (1981), states it well: "An honest man, armed with all the knowledge available to us now, could only state that in some sense, the origin of life appears at the moment to be almost a miracle, so many are the conditions which would have been satisfied to get it going" (88).

43. See Hugh Ross, Kenneth Samples, and Mark Clark, *Lights In The Sky and Little Green Men* (Colorado Springs: NavPress, 2002), 39. See also reasons.org for Hugh Ross's most recent updates on the statistical probabilities involved.

44. C. S. Lewis, *Mere Christianity*.

45. William Lane Craig, *Reasonable Faith, 3rd ed.* (Wheaton, IL: Crossway, 2009).

ABOUT THE AUTHORS

BOBBY HARRINGTON (DMin, Southern Baptist Theological Seminary) is CEO of Renew.org and Discipleship.org, both national disciple making networks. Bobby is the founding and Lead Pastor of Harpeth Christian Church. He is author or coauthor of more than a dozen books on disciple making.

CARL AND ALICIA WILLIAMSON are disciple makers and church planters who both serve as professors at Harding University in Searcy, Arkansas. Carl (DMin, Harding School of Theology) is a professor of discipleship and church planting, and Alicia (MA, MA, Harding School of Theology) is an adjunct professor in Bible and ministry.

Made in USA - North Chelmsford, MA
54921_9781959467212
01.09.2024 1521